Self-servicing Your Car

Self-servicing Your Car aims to take some of the sting out of the ever-rising price of motoring. Car depreciation costs and fuel price increases are factors largely beyond Mr. Everydriver's control; servicing and repair charges need not be. Bill Caldwell's illustrations and text give easy-to-follow, step-by-step instructions covering everything from adjusting the points to bleeding the brakes, including what to look for when buying a secondhand car. The reader will not only increase his motoring know-how and save money, but will feel safe in the knowledge that everything that should be attended to during a service has been carried out.

Thomas Nelson and Sons Ltd
36 Park Street London W1Y 4DE
PO Box 18123 Nairobi Kenya

Thomas Nelson (Australia) Ltd
19-39 Jeffcott Street West Melbourne 3003

Thomas Nelson and Sons (Canada) Ltd
81 Curlew Drive Don Mills Ontario

Thomas Nelson (Nigeria) Ltd
PO Box 336 Apapa Lagos

First published in Great Britain in 1975

Copyright © Bill Caldwell in association with P.A. Features 1975

ISBN 0 17 149028 2

Printed in Great Britain by
Tinling (1973) Ltd.,
Prescot, Merseyside

Self-servicing Your Car

Written and Drawn by Bill Caldwell

NELSON

Contents

How to reduce tyre wear	1
How to use less petrol	2
Check the battery	3
Looking for that oil leak	4
Putting in anti-freeze	5
Buying tyres—radial or crossply?	6
Looking at the petrol/air mixture	7
Buying a used car I: Bodywork	8
Buying a used car II: Rust	9
Buying a used car III: Under the bonnet	10
Buying a used car IV: Behind the wheel	11
Washing the car	12
Alternators—do's and don'ts	13
Safety in the workshop	14
Check and adjust the points	15
Check ignition timing	16
Fix a tubeless tyre puncture	17
The thermostat	18
The cooling system: I	19
The cooling system: II	20
Change the oil filter	21
Slow-running adjustment	22
Sparking plugs	23
Check the fuel supply	24
Starter faults	25
The starter—clean the Bendix drive	26
Fit new high-tension leads	27
Adjust clutch pedal free play	28
Top-up the rear axle	29
Windscreen wipers	30
Fitting a new condenser	31
Prevent battery corrosion	32
Lubricate hinges etc.	33
How to Fit a new fan belt	34
Bleed the brakes	35
How to bleed the clutch	36
The air filter	37
Checking the drive shaft	38
Check and service the dynamo: I	39
Check and service the dynamo: II	40
Body repairs I: Filling rust holes	41
Body repairs II: Filling dents	42
Body repairs III: Spraying	43
Fitting a new headlamp	44
Setting the headlamps	45
Fitting wing mirrors	46
Tracing electrical faults: I	47
Tracing electrical faults: II	48
Adjust the brakes	49
Fit a new exhaust system	50
Fit new disc-brake pads: I	51
Fit new disc-brake pads: II	52
Grease the front suspension	53
Fit new brake shoes: I	54
Fit new brake shoes: II	55
Decoke I: Preparation	56
Decoke II: Remove cylinder head	57
Decoke III: Remove valves	58
Decoke IV: Re-assembly	59
Adjust tappets and valve clearances	60

SELF~SERVICING

HOW TO REDUCE TYRE WEAR

TYRE LIFE CAN BE PROLONGED BY SENSIBLE DRIVING.
REMEMBER–
CONTINUAL HIGH SPEED DRIVING, EXCESSIVE USE OF THE BRAKES, FAST CORNERING AND HARD ACCELERATION GREATLY INCREASE TYRE WEAR.

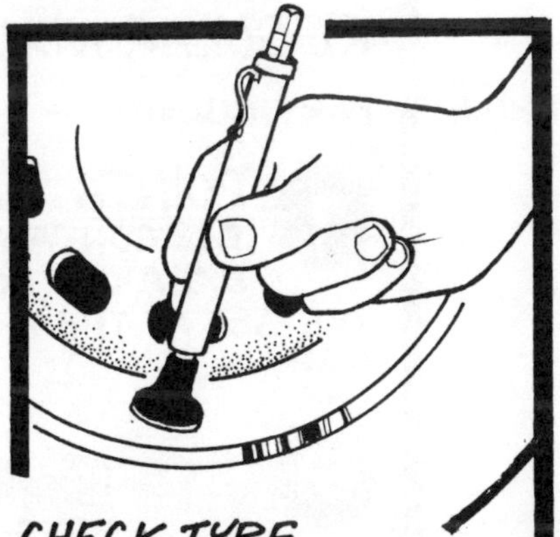

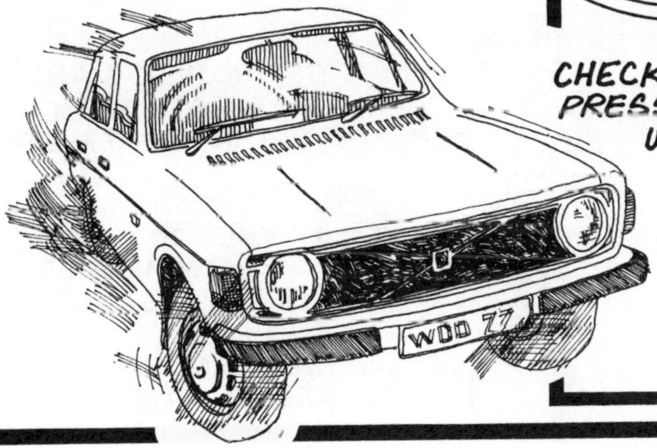

CHECK TYRE PRESSURES EVERY WEEK. A FEW POUNDS BELOW THE RECOMMENDED PRESSURE CAN REDUCE THE TYRE LIFE BY 5,000 MILES OR MORE.

EVEN TYRE WEAR GIVES EVEN TYRE GRIP AND LONGER PERIODS BETWEEN TYRE REPLACEMENTS.

IF ALL FIVE TYRES ARE OF THE SAME TYPE (RADIAL OR CROSSPLY), THIS FIGURE-OF-EIGHT MOVEMENT OF WHEELS EVERY 3,000 MILES WILL HELP TO EQUALISE TYRE WEAR AND GIVE FULL USE OF THE SPARE.

WHILE THE WHEELS ARE OFF, REMOVE STONES LODGED IN THE TYRE TREAD AND EXAMINE FOR UNEVEN OR ABNORMAL WEAR.

FINALLY, ALTER THE TYRE PRESSURES ACCORDING TO THE NEW POSITIONS OF THE WHEELS ON THE CAR.

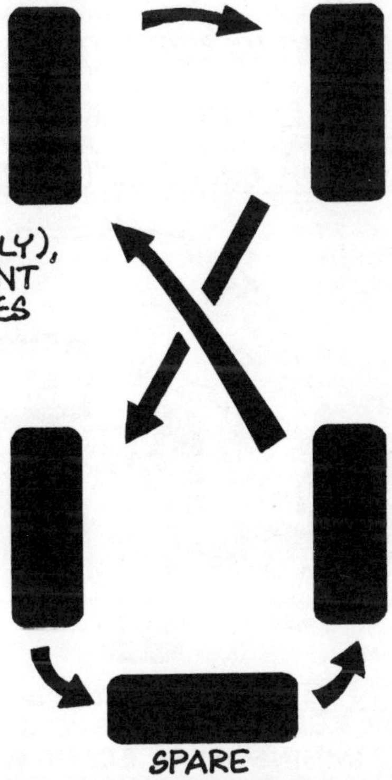

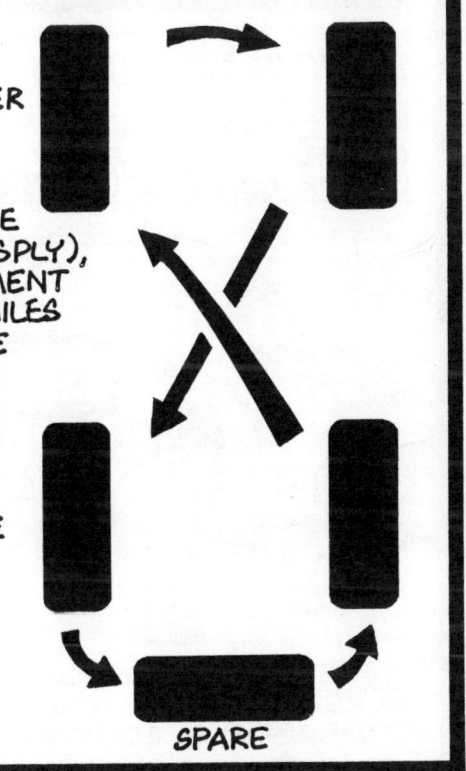

SELF-SERVICING

DRIVING METHOD

<u>WARM ENGINE QUICKLY</u> (A COLD ENGINE USES MORE FUEL) – DRIVE OFF IMMEDIATELY AFTER STARTING.
<u>USE THE CHOKE AS LITTLE AS POSSIBLE</u>.

<u>DRIVE GENTLY</u> – AND WITH ANTICIPATION TO AVOID NEEDLESS STOPPING OR REDUCTION OF SPEED. AVOID HARD ACCELERATION ESPECIALLY WHEN CLIMBING. FUEL ECONOMY IS BEST IN TOP GEAR AT AROUND 30 MPH.

REGULAR MAINTENANCE

PARTICULARLY –

1 <u>POINTS</u>. SEE THAT THE CONTACT BREAKER POINTS ARE SET AT THE PROPER GAP.

2 <u>PLUGS</u>

CLEAN SPARK PLUGS AND CHECK GAPS REGULARLY. REPLACE AFTER 12,000 MILES

3 <u>TYRES</u> KEEP TO THE RECOMMENDED TYRE PRESSURES. AND REDUCE THE CAR'S ROLLING RESISTANCE.

SELF-SERVICING

YOUR CAR BATTERY IS MADE UP OF 6 2 VOLT CELLS JOINED TO GIVE YOU A 12 VOLT BATTERY. IT IS FILLED WITH DILUTE SULPHURIC ACID (ELECTROLYTE). IN USE THIS BECOMES MORE CONCENTRATED AS PART OF THE WATER-CONTENT IS LOST. SO THE LEVEL OF ELECTROLYTE IN THE CELLS FALLS.

YOU SHOULD CHECK YOUR BATTERY ABOUT ONCE A MONTH. REMOVE THE FILLER CAPS AND, IF NECESSARY, TOP-UP WITH DISTILLED WATER. THE FLUID SHOULD JUST COVER THE PLATES. KEEP THE TOPS OF THE CELLS CLEAN.

THE STATE OF CHARGE OF EACH CELL CAN BE TESTED WITH A HYDROMETER. REMOVE THE FILLER CAPS AND USE THE BULB TO SUCK UP ENOUGH ELECTROLYTE TO LIFT THE FLOAT.

HYDROMETER

S.G. 1.000 - 1.150 FLAT

S.G. 1.150 - 1.250 HALF-CHARGE

S.G. 1.250 - 1.285 FULL CHARGE

A DISCHARGED BATTERY MUST BE RECHARGED AT ONCE

MOST BATTERY DIFFICULTIES START WITH THE LEADS. THE TERMINALS SHOULD BE KEPT CLEAN AND FREE FROM CORROSION.
DISCONNECT THE TERMINALS AND USE A WIRE BRUSH TO CLEAN EACH POST AND TERMINAL TO BRIGHTNESS. COAT WITH PETROLEUM JELLY BEFORE RECONNECT-ING. DO THE SAME WITH THE BRAIDED EARTH CONNECTION TO THE CAR BODY.
YOUR BATTERY MAY NEED A FRESHENER CHARGE FROM TIME TO TIME. YOU CAN LEAVE IT ON A TRICKLE CHARGE OVER-NIGHT BUT IF YOUR CAR HAS AN ALTERNATOR DISCONNECT BOTH BATTERY LEADS FIRST.

LOOKING FOR THAT OIL LEAK

EXCESSIVE OIL CONSUMPTION COMBINED WITH AN OILY ENGINE AND OIL DRIPS ON THE GARAGE FLOOR COULD MEAN YOU HAVE AN OIL LEAK.

TO FIND EXACTLY WHERE THE OIL IS COMING FROM :-

CLEAN THE ENGINE WITH PARAFFIN -SOAKED RAGS. AND, AFTER ALLOWING THE PARAFFIN TO DRY OFF, TAKE THE CAR FOR A FIVE MILE DRIVE. THEN CHECK THE ENGINE OVER CARE- FULLY. LEAKS FROM THE AREAS SHOWN SHOULD THEN BE EASILY SEEN .

ROCKER COVER

CYLINDER HEAD

SUMP

SUMP DRAIN PLUG

CRANKSHAFT BEARING

THE REMEDY FOR MOST OF THESE LEAKS IS TO TIGHTEN THE JOINT OR FIT A NEW GASKET.

TAKE CARE WHEN MAKING A NEW JOINT THAT BOTH SURFACES ARE CLEAN AND USE JOINTING COMPOUND IF NECESSARY.

WHERE THE LEAKING IS NOT DUE TO FAULTY JOINTS IT IS LIKELY TO BE FROM THE CRANKSHAFT BEARING THIS IS CAUSED BY FAULTY OIL SEALS OR BEARING WEAR.

SELF~SERVICING

IF THE COOLING WATER FREEZES IN COLD WEATHER YOU COULD END UP WITH A CRACKED RADIATOR – OR WORSE. TO PREVENT THIS, ANTI-FREEZE IS ADDED TO THE COOLANT – USUALLY 25% BY VOLUME

3 PARTS WATER TO 1 ANTIFREEZE

BEFORE ADDING ANTI-FREEZE CHECK ALL HOSES AND JOINTS. THEY MUST BE SOUND BECAUSE ANTI-FREEZE 'SEARCHES OUT' THE SMALLEST LEAKS IN THE COOLING SYSTEM.

ANTI-FREEZE LOWERS THE FREEZING POINT OF THE COOLANT. BUT IT ALSO RAISES ITS *BOILING POINT* – SO YOU BENEFIT BY LEAVING IT IN ALL YEAR.

212°F (100°C)

32°F (0°C)

BOILING POINT WITH ANTI-FREEZE

FREEZING POINT WITH ANTI-FREEZE

REMOVE THE RADIATOR CAP, DRAIN THE SYSTEM AND, USING A HOSE, FLUSH THE SYSTEM THROUGH.

CLOSE THE TAPS AND HALF-FILL THE SYSTEM WITH WATER. THEN ADD THE ANTI-FREEZE.

RUN THE ENGINE FOR A FEW MINUTES BEFORE TOPPING-UP.

5

SELF-SERVICING

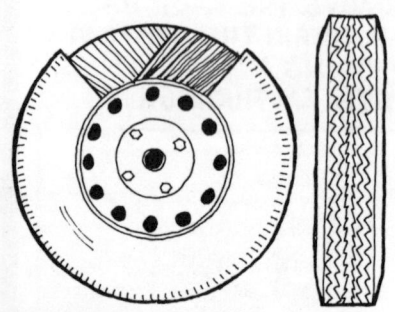

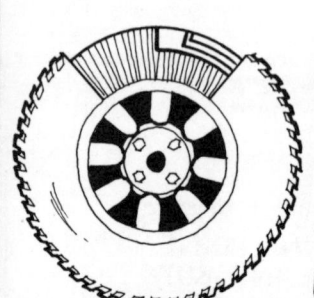

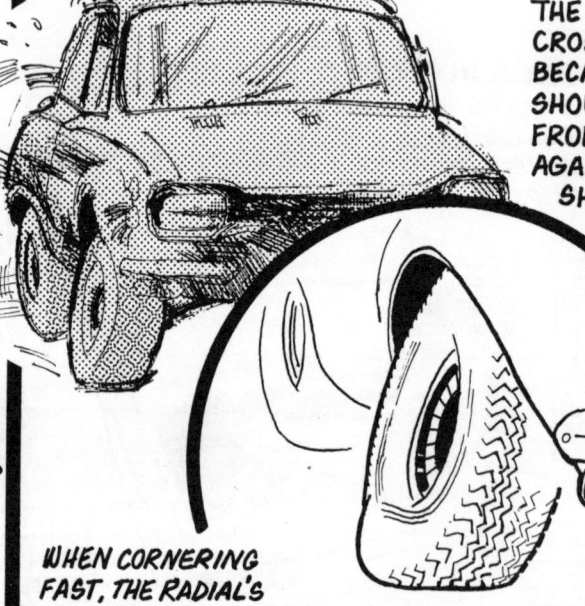

CROSSPLY TYRES HAVE CASINGS MADE FROM RAYON POLYESTER LAID IN DIAGONAL LAYERS ACROSS THE TYRE. THE TREAD IS USUALLY A BLEND OF SYNTHETIC RUBBER DESIGNED FOR GOOD GRIP, QUIET AND COOL RUNNING. THEY'RE CHEAPER THAN RADIALS, BUT SINCE MILEAGE IS MUCH LESS COST PER-MILE IS HIGHER.

ON **RADIAL PLY TYRES** THE LAYERS RUN FROM BEAD TO BEAD ACROSS THE TYRE AT RIGHT ANGLES. THIS GIVES GREATER PLIABILITY. THE TREAD IS MADE VERY FIRM BY CORDS RUNNING ROUND THE TYRE BENEATH THE TREAD. THESE CORDS ARE USUALLY SPUN FROM RAYON OR, BECOMING MORE POPULAR, FINE STEEL WIRE.

WHEN CORNERING FAST, THE RADIAL'S FLEXIBLE WALLS ALLOW THE WHOLE TREAD TO STAY FLAT. THIS GIVES A MUCH BETTER GRIP.

THE SAME TYPE MUST BE FITTED ON THE SAME AXLE - RADIAL WITH RADIAL, CROSSPLY WITH CROSSPLY. BECAUSE RADIALS GRIP BETTER, THEY SHOULD _NEVER_ BE FITTED ON THE FRONT WHEELS ONLY (IT IS ALSO AGAINST THE LAW). ALL FOUR WHEELS SHOULD HAVE EITHER RADIALS OR CROSSPLYS. IF YOU _MUST_ MIX THEM, REMEMBER -
RADIALS ON THE REAR

SIZE MARKING. GENERALLY TYRES SHOW TWO SIZE MARKINGS - THE WIDTH OF THE TYRE AND THE DIAMETER OF THE WHEEL. E.G. 520×10 MEANS 5·2" WIDE TYRE ON A 10" WHEEL. ON RADIALS THE WIDTH OF THE TYRE IS IN M.M,s AND THE WHEEL DIAMETER IN INCHES. EG. 145×13 .

SELF~SERVICING

THE CORRECT RATIO OF AIR TO PETROL FOR COMPLETE COMBUSTION IS AROUND 15 PARTS OF AIR TO ONE OF PETROL BY WEIGHT.
THE CARBURETTOR, OF COURSE, VARIES THE PROPORTIONS FOR SUCH DIFFERENT OPERATING CONDITIONS AS COLD STARTING, IDLING, CRUISING AND ACCELERATION.

HERE ARE SOME OF THE SYMPTOMS AND CAUSES OF A WEAK (SMALLER PETROL/AIR RATIO) MIXTURE.

SYMPTOMS OF A WEAK MIXTURE

1 ENGINE OVERHEATS

2 SPITTING BACK THROUGH THE CARBURETTOR

3 ENGINE LACKS POWER

4 WHITE DEPOSIT ON PLUGS

POSSIBLE CAUSES OF A WEAK MIXTURE

1 WRONG CARBURETTOR ADJUSTMENT.
2 AIR LEAK BETWEEN THE CARBURETTOR AND THE ENGINE.
3 WORN VALVE GUIDES ALLOWING AIR TO BE DRAWN INTO THE ENGINE WITHOUT GOING THROUGH THE CARBURETTOR.
4 A CHOKED PETROL FILTER OR A FAULTY FUEL PUMP.
5 WATER IN THE PETROL.

SELF~SERVICING

BUYING A USED CAR I: BODYWORK

IF POSSIBLE, GET AN INDEPENDENT REPORT ON A CAR'S CONDITION (FROM A MOTORING ORGANISATION OR SPECIALIST FIRM) BEFORE BUYING.
MANY CARS SUFFER ACCIDENT DAMAGE, ARE PROPERLY REPAIRED AND CARRY ON GIVING GOOD SERVICE FOR YEARS. OTHERS ARE JUST PATCHED UP AND RESPRAYED. IN EITHER CASE YOU WANT TO KNOW BUT YOU CAN'T GET A REPORT ON EVERY CAR YOU LOOK AT. HERE ARE 4 POINTS TO HELP YOU IN THE SELECTION PROCESS –

VIEW THE CAR FROM A DISTANCE AND SEE IF YOU CAN DETECT ANY MISMATCH OF COLOUR (SHOWING PARTIAL RESPRAY).

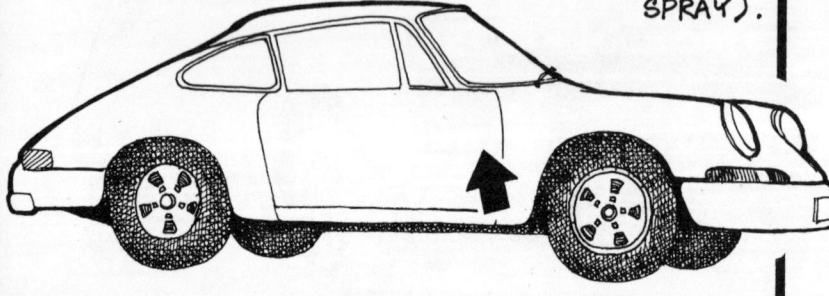

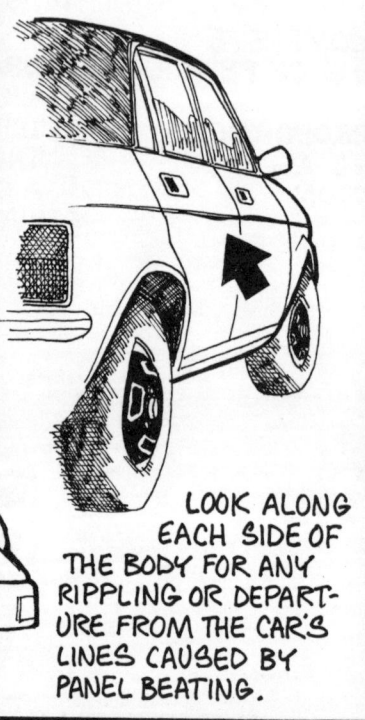

LOOK ALONG EACH SIDE OF THE BODY FOR ANY RIPPLING OR DEPARTURE FROM THE CAR'S LINES CAUSED BY PANEL BEATING.

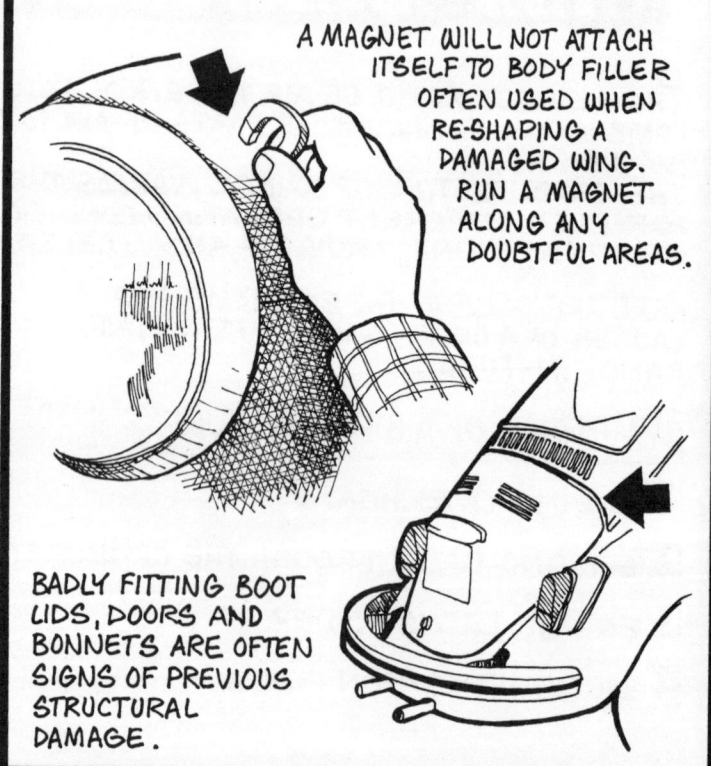

A MAGNET WILL NOT ATTACH ITSELF TO BODY FILLER OFTEN USED WHEN RE-SHAPING A DAMAGED WING. RUN A MAGNET ALONG ANY DOUBTFUL AREAS.

BADLY FITTING BOOT LIDS, DOORS AND BONNETS ARE OFTEN SIGNS OF PREVIOUS STRUCTURAL DAMAGE.

8

SELF~SERVICING

LOOK FOR RUST

RUST TARNISH AND RUST ROT (IF NOT TOO EXTENSIVE) CAN BE CLEANED UP. BUT IT ALWAYS ALWAYS COMES BACK AND COSTS YOU MONEY THROUGH DEPRECIATION, IN REPAIRS TO KEEP UP THE CAR'S APPEARANCE AND, EVENTUALLY, TO KEEP THE CAR ROADWORTHY.

1 SLIGHT TARNISH COMMON IN 2-3 YEAR OLD CARS BUT NOT ALWAYS OBVIOUS IN A SHOWROOM SETTING.
IF EXTENSIVE, BODYWORK HAS BEEN NEGLECTED. IT'S LIKELY, THEREFORE, THAT GENERAL MAINTENANCE HAS NOT BEEN CARRIED OUT REGULARLY.

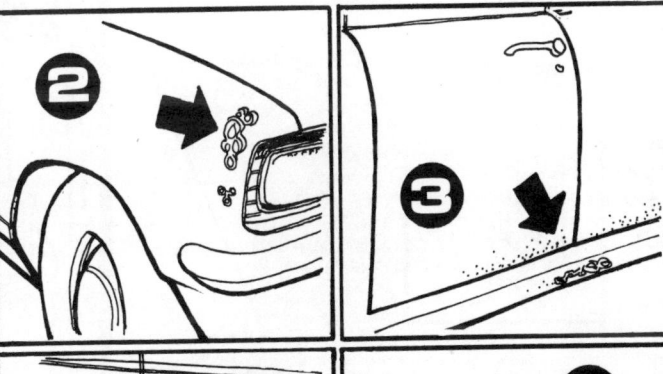

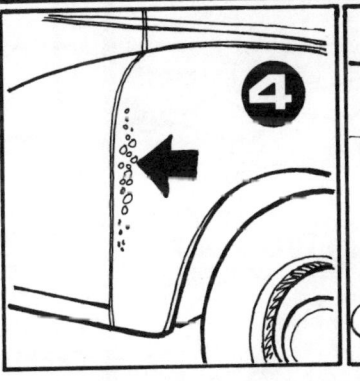

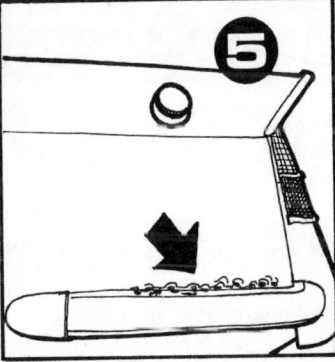

2 ROAD DIRT GETS INTO THE CAVITIES BEHIND THE HEADLAMPS. WHEN RUST BREAKS THROUGH THE PAINT SURFACE IT MEANS THE PANEL IS RUSTING AWAY FROM THE INSIDE. IT'S CERTAIN THAT OTHER LESS ACCESSIBLE PANELS AND BOX SECTIONS ARE GOING THE SAME WAY.

3 DOOR BOTTOMS AND DOOR SILLS OF ALMOST ALL CARS GO THIS WAY EVENTUALLY.

4 BUBBLING PAINTWORK IS A FORERUNNER TO ② AND SHOULD BE TAKEN SERIOUSLY.

5 EVERY MAKE OF CAR HAS AT LEAST ONE RUST TRAP OR SPOT WHERE RUST GETS A HOLD FIRST. FIND OUT WHERE THIS IS ON THE MODEL YOU'RE LOOKING FOR.

COOLING SYSTEM

WITH THE ENGINE COLD, CHECK THE RADIATOR (A) TOP HOSE (B) AND BOTTOM HOSE (C) FOR LEAKS (WHICH MAY SHOW AS ANTI-FREEZE STAINS). EXPECT SOME RUST ON THE RAD. BUT A HEAVILY RUSTED ONE

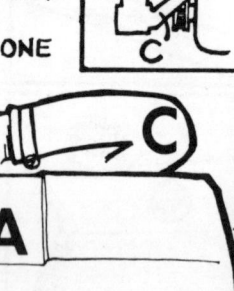

ALSO CHECK THE HEATER HOSES.

IS INEFFICIENT AND IS LIKELY TO CAUSE TROUBLE SO ALSO WILL OVERSOFT OR BRITTLE HOSES.

HYDRAULIC SYSTEM

CHECK FLUID LEVELS IN THE BRAKE AND CLUTCH HYDRAULIC RESERVOIRS. AND LOOK AT BRAKE HOSES AND PIPES FOR LEAKS OR SIGNS OF CHAFING OR PERISHING.

WIRING

CRACKED, FRAYED AND NEGLECTED WIRING WILL CAUSE ELECTRICAL FAILURES AND COSTLY BREAKDOWNS

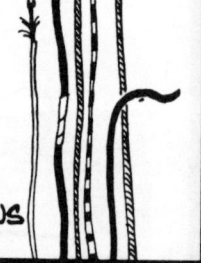

OIL LEAKS

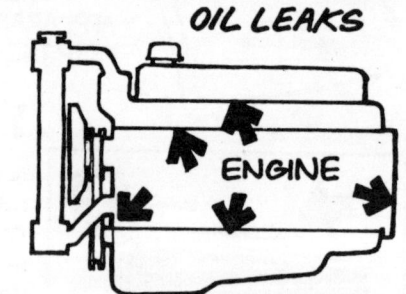

ENGINE

EXAMINE THESE AREAS BEFORE AND AFTER A 15 MINUTE TEST DRIVE. *SLIGHT* TRACES OF OIL ON THE ENGINE ARE NORMAL.

SELF-SERVICING

IF POSSIBLE, TEST DRIVE THE CAR YOU'RE THINKING OF BUYING. TRY IT FOR COMFORT AND PERFORMANCE. AND SEE IF THE GENERAL NOISE LEVEL AND VIBRATION ARE NOT MORE THAN YOU EXPECT.

THE OIL WARNING AND IGNITION LIGHTS

THEY SHOULD GO OUT AFTER YOU START THE ENGINE. IF THEY DON'T, EXPECT TROUBLE WITH OIL PRESSURE OR THE GENERATOR.

STEERING

MOVE THE WHEEL WHILE LOOKING AT THE ROAD WHEELS. THE PLAY BEFORE THE WHEELS ARE MOVED SHOULD NOT BE MORE THAN 1"-2".

SWITCHES AND ACCESSORIES

CHECK THAT ALL LIGHTS, INDICATORS HORN, WIPERS, HEATER AND RADIO ETC. ARE IN GOOD WORKING ORDER.

THE BRAKE PEDAL SHOULD FEEL FIRM AND HAVE LITTLE FREE TRAVEL.
THE CLUTCH SHOULD ENGAGE SMOOTHLY AND WITHOUT GRAB.

SELF-SERVICING

WASHING THE CAR

TO MAKE A GOOD JOB OF WASHING THE CAR THEREBY KEEPING UP ITS GOOD APPEARANCE AND PRESERVING THE PAINTWORK —

- DO IT REGULARLY
- DO IT IN THE SHADE OR ON A DULL DAY
- USE PLENTY OF WATER

START WITH THE ROOF AND FLOAT THE DUST AWAY WITH A SPRAY OF CLEAN WATER. THEN, WITH A BUCKET OF WARM SOAPY WATER, WASH THE CAR IN THE SEQUENCE SHOWN. RINSE WELL AS YOU GO ALONG.

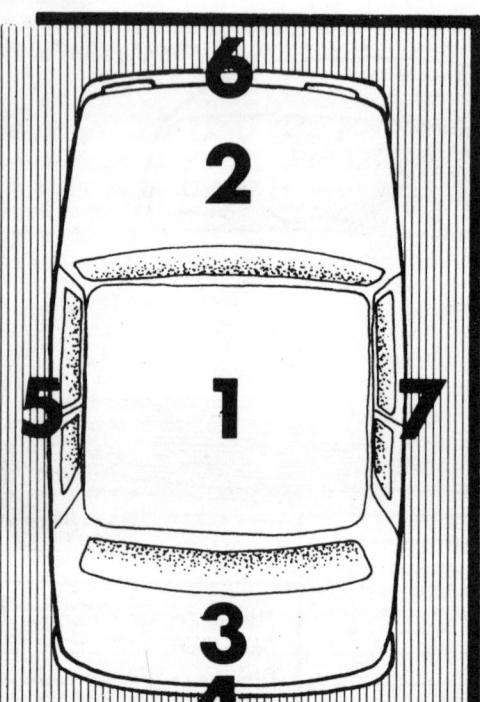

WASH AND DRY RAIN CHANNELS, RADIATOR GRILLES, HEADLAMPS, REAR LIGHTS, REFLECTORS, NUMBER PLATES ETC.

WIPER BLADES SHOULD BE CLEANED WITH A DIFFERENT SPONGE TO MAKE CERTAIN NO GREASE OR POLISH GETS ON THEM. CLEAN THEM WITH SCREEN-WASH FLUID.

WHEELS ARE OFTEN FORGOTTEN. WASH THEM LAST. DO THE HUB CAPS, WHEEL RIMS AND TYRE WALLS. AND SEE HOW MUCH SMARTER THE CAR LOOKS.

FOR THE WINDOWS TAKE A CLEAN CHAMOIS LEATHER WITH CLEAN WATER AND A SPOT OF METHYLATED SPIRIT.
USE METHS ALSO TO REMOVE TAR SPOTS AND RINSE WITH CLEAN WATER.

SELF-SERVICING

ALTERNATORS – DO'S AND DON'TS

DOES YOUR CAR HAVE AN ALTERNATOR?
MANY MODERN CARS ARE NOW
FITTED WITH ALTERNATORS BECAUSE
THEY CAN SUPPLY CURRENT
MORE EASILY FOR THE EVER-
INCREASING NUMBER OF
ELECTRICAL ACCESSORIES
FITTED TO CARS.

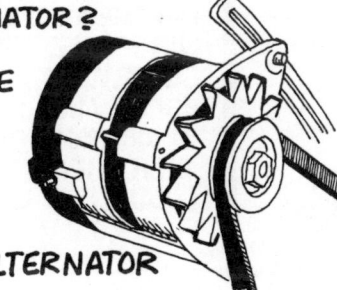

ALTERNATOR

SPECIAL CARE, HOWEVER,
IS NEEDED WHEN
DEALING WITH AN
ALTERNATOR. IT IS <u>NOT</u>
A DIFFERENT KIND OF
DYNAMO. AND IT IS
EASILY DAMAGED WHERE
A DYNAMO WOULD NOT
BE.
HERE ARE SOME DO'S
AND DON'TS—

Do

MAKE PERIODIC CHECKS
ON THE DRIVE BELT.
IT MUST BE KEPT AT
EXACTLY THE CORRECT
TENSION.

CHECK CAREFULLY
BEFORE CONNECTING
UP THE BATTERY.
REVERSED
CONNECTIONS WILL
DAMAGE THE
ALTERNATOR.

CHECK CONNECTIONS IN
THE ALTERNATOR CIRCUIT,
BATTERY TERMINALS
AND EARTH CONNECTIONS.
A BROKEN OR DIRTY
CONNECTION WILL CAUSE
AN OVERLOAD.

Don't ...

RUN THE ENGINE
WITH THE BATTERY
DISCONNECTED (NOT
EVEN FOR A MOMENT).

CHARGE THE BATTERY
WITHOUT FIRST
DISCONNECTING BOTH
LEADS.

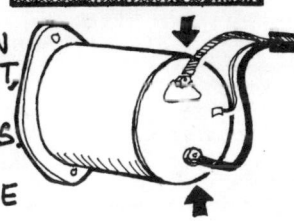

USE ELECTRIC DRILLS,
SOLDERING IRON ETC
ON THE CAR WITHOUT
FIRST ISOLATING THE
ALTERNATOR.

SELF-SERVICING

SAFETY IN THE WORKSHOP

DON'T DEPEND ON JACKS ALONE WHEN WORKING UNDER THE CAR. A HARD TUG ON A STUBBORN NUT CAN MAKE THE CAR ROLL OFF THE JACKS. PILES OF BRICKS ARE EVEN MORE DANGEROUS. AXLE STANDS OR STEEL RAMPS ARE THE BEST WAY FOR THE HOME MECHANIC TO PROVIDE A RIGID BASE WHICH IS NOT EASILY DISTURBED.

DON'T FORGET THE FINAL TIGHTENING OF WHEEL NUTS AFTER REPLACING A WHEEL.

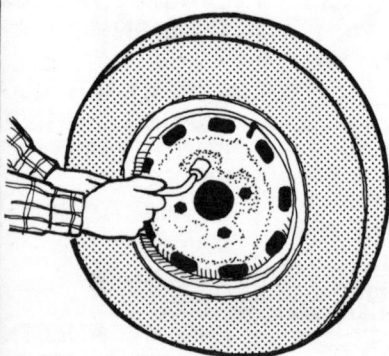

CHECK OVER CAREFULLY ANY WORK YOU HAVE DONE ON THE CAR BEFORE TAKING IT OUT TO TEST.

DON'T USE UN-EARTHED OR BADLY WIRED ELECTRICAL EQUIPMENT. IT IS ESPECIALLY RISKY IN WORKSHOPS WITH THEIR (USUALLY) WET FLOORS.

DON'T USE LARGE QUANTITIES OF PARAFFIN OR PETROL FOR CLEANING IN ENCLOSED AREAS. ALWAYS DISCONNECT THE BATTERY IF THERE IS A CHANCE OF ELECTRICAL SHORTING. ALWAYS KEEP A FIRE EXTINGUISHER OR ASBESTOS BLANKET IN THE WORKSHOP.

SELF-SERVICING

SIGNS & SYMPTOMS

IF YOUR CAR'S PERFORMANCE IS SLUGGISH OR UNEVEN, IT COULD BE WORTH YOUR WHILE TO CHECK AND ADJUST THE POINTS

TOOLS FOR THE JOB

SCREWDRIVER
FEELER GUAGES

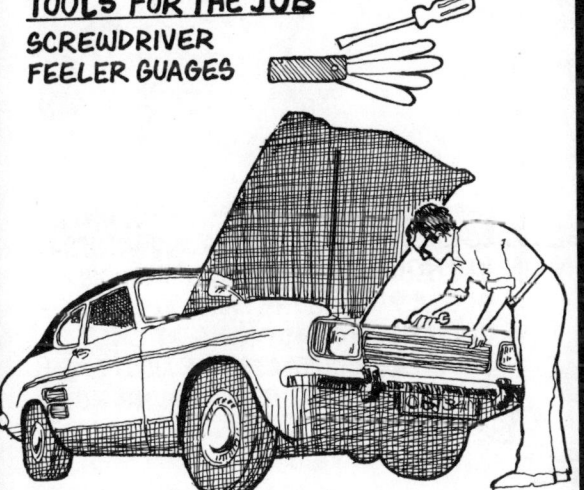

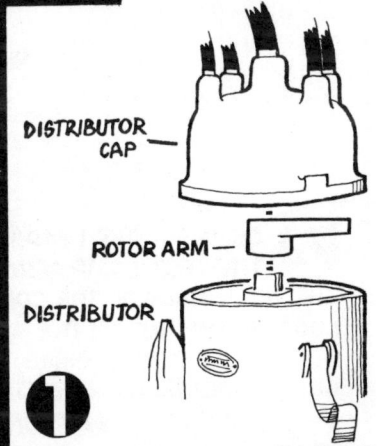

DISTRIBUTOR CAP —

ROTOR ARM —

DISTRIBUTOR —

❶ REMOVE THE DISTRIBUTOR CAP AND ROTOR ARM. EXAMINE THE CONDITION OF THE POINTS BY OPENING THEM WITH A FINGER.
AFTER SEVERAL THOUSAND MILES IT IS COMMON FOR A PIP TO FORM ON ONE POINT AND A CORRESPONDING HOLLOW TO APPEAR IN THE OPPOSITE POINT. IF DEEPLY PITTED, REPLACE.

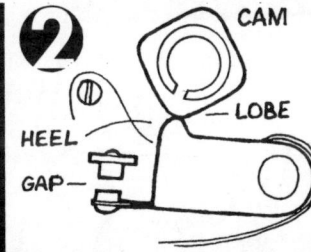

CAM

LOBE

HEEL
GAP —

❷ TO SET THE GAP (USUALLY 0·015" OR 0·025"- SEE HANDBOOK). REMOVE THE SPARKING PLUGS AND TURN ENGINE OVER WITH A SPANNER ON THE CRANKSHAFT PULLEY NUT. STOP WHEN THE PLASTIC HEEL IS RESTING ON ONE OF THE CAM LOBES -THE GAP BETWEEN THE POINTS IS THEN AT ITS MAXIMUM. USE FEELER GUAGES TO CHECK THE GAP.

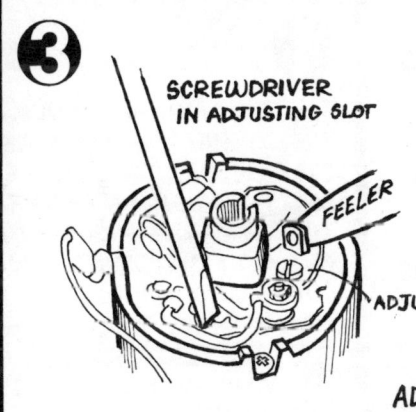

SCREWDRIVER IN ADJUSTING SLOT

FEELER

ADJUSTING SCREW

❸ NOW SLACKEN THE ADJUSTING SCREW AND INSERT A SCREWDRIVER INTO THE SLOT PROVIDED. TWIST THE SCREWDRIVER TO OPEN OR CLOSE THE GAP. WHEN THE CLEARANCE IS JUST RIGHT THERE IS A SLIGHT DRAG ON THE FEELER BLADE. TIGHTEN THE ADJUSTING SCREW AND CHECK THE GAP.

AFTER MAKING ADJUSTMENTS TO CONTACT BREAKER POINTS IT IS ADVISABLE TO CHECK THE IGNITION TIMING. FOR A STEP-BY-STEP GUIDE SEE NEXT PANEL OF SELF-SERVICING.

SELF-SERVICING

CHECK IGNITION TIMING

SIGNS & SYMPTOMS

WHEN THE ENGINE MISFIRES, OR THE PERFORMANCE IS BELOW PAR, YOUR FIRST CHECK SHOULD BE THE IGNITION SYSTEM (WE DID THE POINTS LAST PANEL*)

TOOLS FOR THE JOB

TIMING LIGHT
(12 volt BULB & TWO WIRES WITH CROC. CLIPS)

A LARGE SPANNER TO FIT CRANKSHAFT PULLEY NUT
(FOR TURNING ENGINE OVER)

A SMALL SPANNER TO FIT DISTRIBUTOR RETAINING NUT

* PLEASE NOTE

THE ENGINE MUST BE COLD. AND BEFORE CHECKING OR SETTING IGNITION TIMING ALWAYS SET POINTS TO THE CORRECT GAP

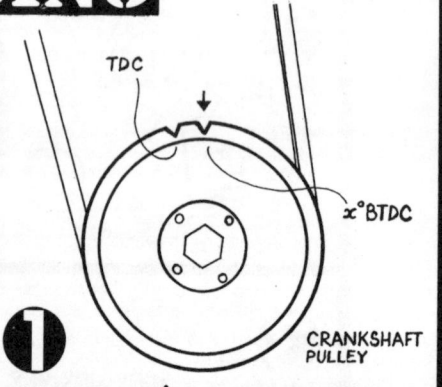

1 SEE THE CAR'S HANDBOOK FOR THE CORRECT IGNITION TIMING (IN ° BEFORE TOP DEAD CENTRE) AND THE POSITION OF THE TIMING MARKS — USUALLY A MARK ON THE TIMING CHAIN COVER AND NOTCHES ON THE CRANKSHAFT PULLEY. TURN THE ENGINE OVER UNTIL THE MARK AND (USUALLY) THE RIGHT-HAND NOTCH ARE IN LINE.

TDC

$x°$BTDC

CRANKSHAFT PULLEY

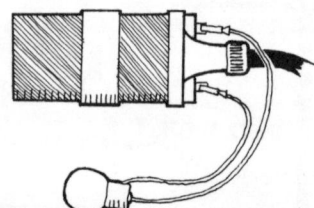

2 CONNECT THE LEADS OF THE TEST LAMP ACROSS THE TERMINALS OF THE COIL. LOOSEN THE NUT ON THE DISTRIBUTOR RETAINING CLAMP AND SWITCH ON THE IGNITION.

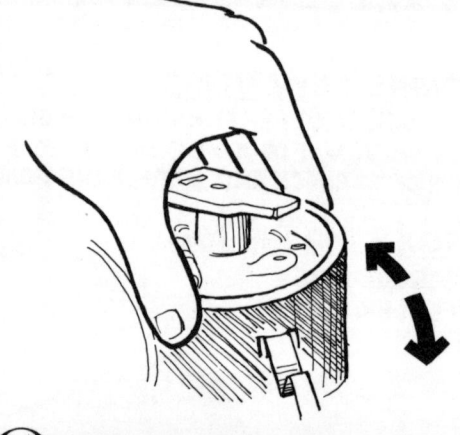

3 TURN THE DISTRIBUTOR UNTIL THE LAMP LIGHTS. NOW TURN THE BODY THE OPPOSITE WAY VERY SLOWLY UNTIL THE LAMP JUST GOES OUT AND STOP TURNING AT ONCE. THE CONTACTS ARE NOW OPEN. TIGHTEN THE RETAINING NUT AND RE-CHECK.

SELF-SERVICING

FIX A TUBELESS TYRE PUNCTURE

TOOLS FOR THE JOB

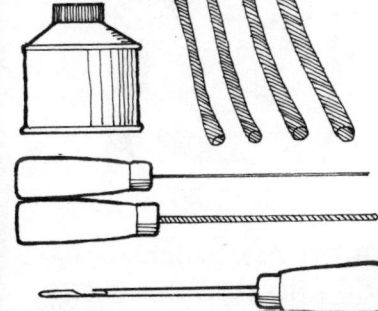

PUNCTURE REPAIRS CAN BE MADE QUICKLY WITH THE TYRE ON THE WHEEL. A REPAIR KIT CONTAINS—
RUBBER SOLUTION; PLUGS; WIRE PROBE; RASP AND PLUGGING TOOL.

1 REMOVE THE OBJECT WHICH CAUSED THE PUNCTURE AND—

2 USE THE WIRE PROBE OR RASP (FOR RADIALS) TO FIND THE SIZE AND DIRECTION OF THE HOLE.

1+2

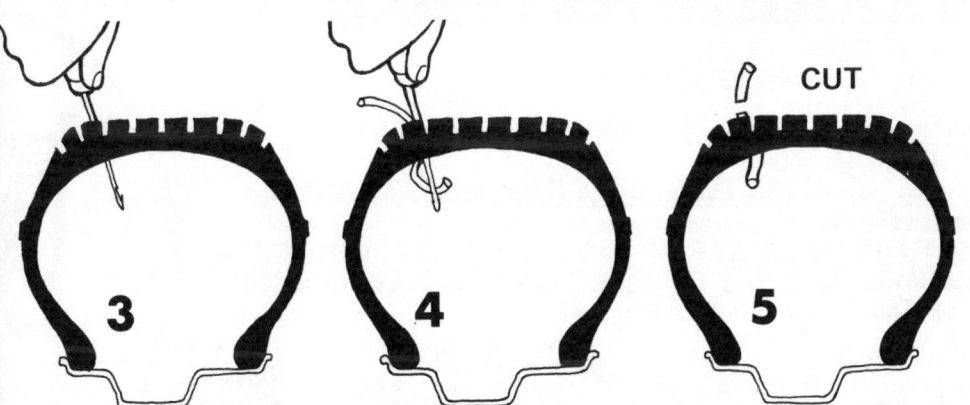

CUT

3 REMOVE THE PROBE, DIP THE PLUGGING TOOL IN THE SOLUTION AND WORK IT INTO THE HOLE.

4 FIX A RUBBER PLUG INTO THE EYE OF THE PLUGGING TOOL. DIP THEM IN THE SOLUTION AND PUSH THE TOOL –WITH THE PLUG–THROUGH THE HOLE, TWISTING IF NECESSARY.

5 REMOVE THE TOOL AND CUT OFF EXCESS PLUG ABOVE THE SURFACE OF THE TYRE. INFLATE TO FULL PRESSURE AND THE TYRE IS READY FOR IMMEDIATE USE.

NB A VULCANISED REPAIR SHOULD BE MADE AS SOON AS POSSIBLE AFTER THIS 'TEMPORARY MEASURE'.

SELF-SERVICING

SOME COMMON FAULTS –

JAMMING IN THE OPEN POSITION AND CAUSING COLD RUNNING.

JAMMING IN THE CLOSED POSITION CAUSING OVER-HEATING.

TEST FOR LATTER BY RUNNING TEMPORARILY WITHOUT THE THERMOSTAT. IF THE TROUBLE DISAPPEARS YOU'LL KNOW IT IS FAULTY. BUY AND FIT A NEW ONE.

TO REMOVE THE THERMO-STAT, DRAIN THE SYSTEM TO AT LEAST THE TOP HOSE CONNECTION. UNDO THE HOUSING AND LIFT OUT THE THERMOSTAT.

CHECK WITH YOUR CAR'S HANDBOOK THAT YOU HAVE THE RIGHT 'STAT FOR YOUR CAR. THE TEMPERATURE AT WHICH IT SHOULD OPEN IS MARKED ON IT.

A THERMOSTAT CAN CAUSE TROUBLE BY OPENING AND CLOSING AT THE WRONG TEMPERATURES. CHECK THIS BY HEATING IT UP SUSPENDED IN A PAN OF WATER.

THE THERMOSTAT SHOULD START TO OPEN AT ITS RATED TEMPERATURE AND OPEN FULLY AS THE TEMPERATURE RISES FURTHER. SEE ALSO THAT IT CLOSES AS THE WATER COOLS.

SELF-SERVICING

SIGNS & SYMPTOMS

YOUR CAR CAN OVERHEAT FOR A NUMBER OF REASONS INCLUDING WRONG PLUGS, PRE-IGNITION, OVER-ADVANCED IGNITION AND SLACK FAN BELT.

IT CAN ALSO BE AN INEFFICIENT COOLING SYSTEM.

AIR PASSES THROUGH THE RADIATOR COOLING THE METAL HONEYCOMB AND THE WATER (COOLANT) PUMPING THROUGH IT.

AN INEFFICIENT RADIATOR MAY BE—

① PREVENTING AIR COOLING THE HONEYCOMB IF IT IS BLOCKED WITH INSECTS AND ROAD FILTH. OR

② STOPPING THE FREE-FLOW OF WATER BY A BUILD UP OF SCALE AND DEPOSIT INSIDE.

OR BOTH ① & ② .

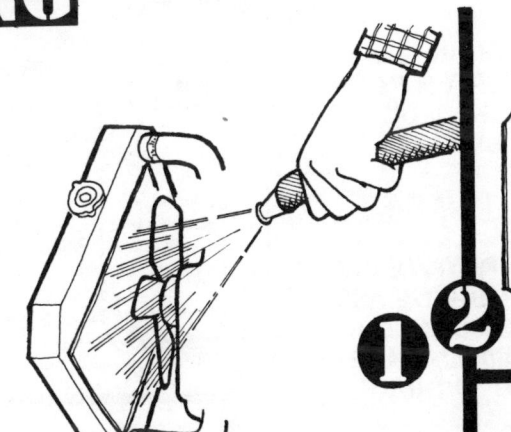

CAP

TOP HOSE

BOTTOM HOSE

① ②

COVER THE ENGINE WITH A PLASTIC SHEET. AND HOSE THE RADIATOR THROUGH FROM BEHIND. YOU CAN TEST THE EFFECT BY SHINING A LAMP THROUGH FROM BEHIND. FOR STUBBORN RUST OR GREASE, BRUSH ON A SOLVENT AND HOSE.

DRAIN THE RAD. AND FLUSH THROUGH. BUT FOR STUB-BORN DIRT AND SCALE, BACK FLUSH. CONNECT THE GARDEN HOSE TO THE RAD'S BOTTOM HOSE AND TURN ON FULL PRESSURE. A PIECE OF CYCLE INNER TUBE FITTED TO THE TOP HOSE WILL HELP DIRECT THE DIRTY WATER AWAY.

FOR REALLY HEAVY FOULING, BEFORE BACK-FLUSHING DRIVE FOR A FEW MILES WITH A WASHING SODA SOL-UTION (OR FLUSHING MIXTURE) IN THE SYSTEM. BUT ONLY IF YOUR RAD. IS SOUND.

MORE ON THE COOLING SYSTEM NEXT PANEL

19

SELF-SERVICING

THE COOLING SYSTEM II

SIGNS & SYMPTOMS

DID YOU CHECK THE WATER IN YOUR RADIATOR TODAY? SHORTAGE OF WATER IS A COMMON CAUSE OF OVER-HEATING, OWING TO THE DRIVER NOT TOPPING-UP OR A LEAK IN THE SYSTEM. IF YOU FIND YOU HAVE TO TOP-UP FREQUENTLY CHECK FOR LEAKS :—

1 LOOK FOR SIGNS OF OIL IN THE COOLING WATER OR WATER IN THE OIL (DROPS ON THE DIPSTICK) INDICATING LEAKAGE FROM A FAULTY CYLINDER HEAD GASKET.
WATCH, ALSO, FOR DRIPS FROM THE WATER PUMP.

2 TOP & BOTTOM HOSES. REMOVE AND EXAMINE THOROUGHLY INSIDE AND OUT FOR DAMAGE OR DETERIORATION.

3 WORM DRIVE CLIPS SHOULD MAKE A TIGHT, SECURE JOINT WITHOUT CUTTING INTO THE HOSE.

4 THE RADIATOR CAP WITH ITS SPRING-LOADED VALVE KEEPS THE SYSTEM UNDER PRESSURE TO RAISE THE BOILING POINT OF THE WATER. A FAULTY VALVE WILL ALLOW WATER TO ESCAPE THRO' THE OVER-FLOW. HAVE IT PRESSURE TESTED OR REPLACE WITH ONE OF THE SAME PRESSURE RATING.

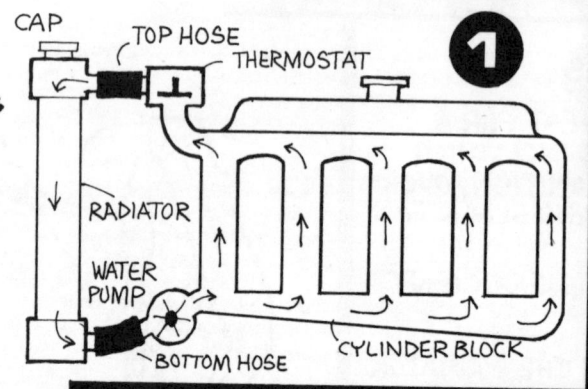

CAP · TOP HOSE · THERMOSTAT · RADIATOR · WATER PUMP · BOTTOM HOSE · CYLINDER BLOCK

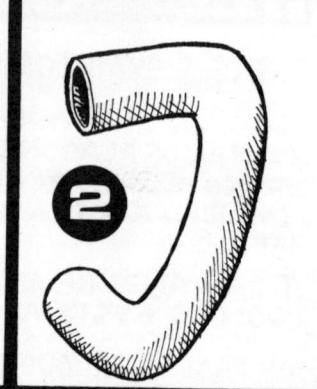

SELF-SERVICING

CHANGE THE OIL FILTER

A CLOGGED OIL FILTER WILL RESTRICT OIL CIRCULATION AND CAUSE LOW OIL PRESSURE. SO REMEMBER TO CHANGE THE OIL FILTER EVERY SECOND TIME YOU DO AN OIL CHANGE. THERE ARE TWO MAIN TYPES OF OIL FILTER — THE ELEMENT FILTER WHICH FITS INTO A BOWL BOLTED ONTO THE ENGINE. THE CARTRIDGE FILTER — ELEMENT AND THROW-AWAY BOWL IN ONE.

UNSCREW THE SECURING SCREW, [1] REMOVE THE BOLT

AND [2] WITHDRAW THE FILTER BOWL.

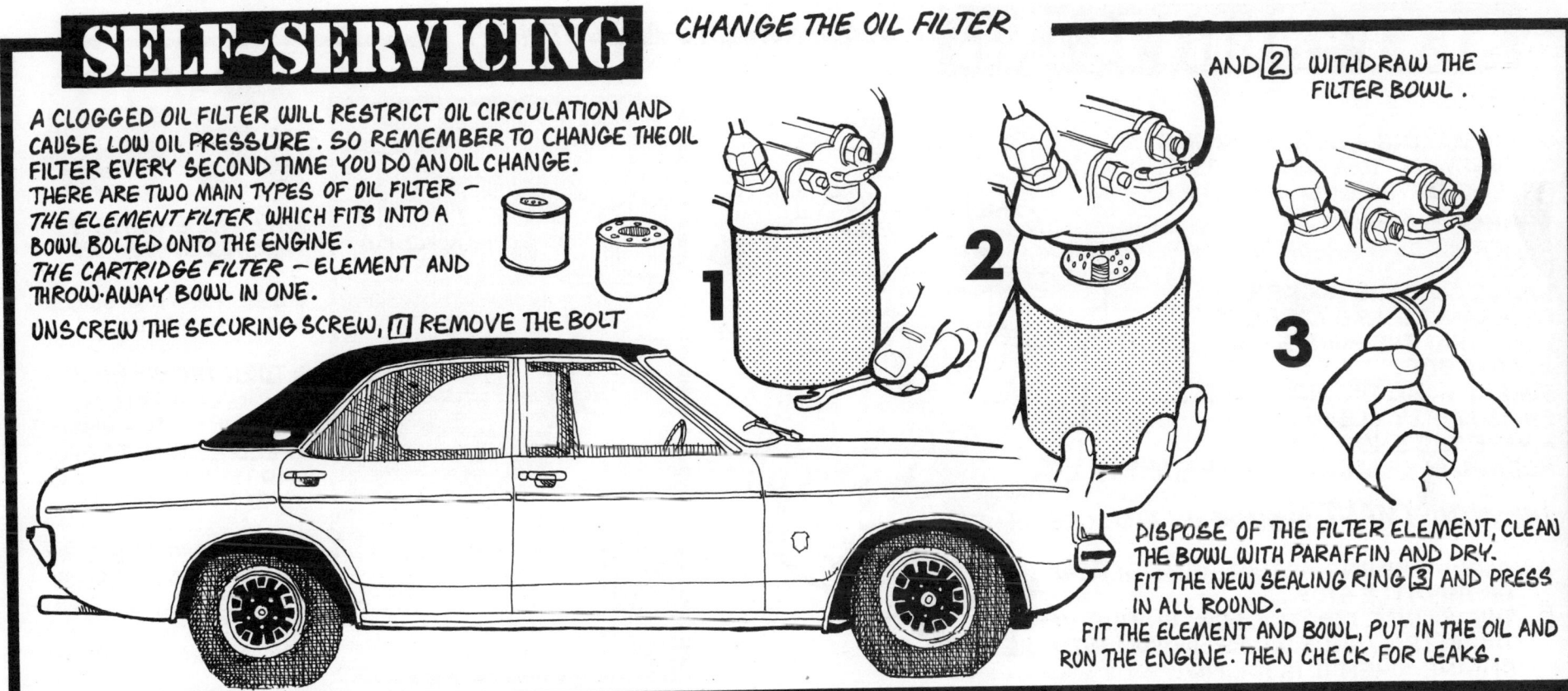

DISPOSE OF THE FILTER ELEMENT, CLEAN THE BOWL WITH PARAFFIN AND DRY. FIT THE NEW SEALING RING [3] AND PRESS IN ALL ROUND. FIT THE ELEMENT AND BOWL, PUT IN THE OIL AND RUN THE ENGINE. THEN CHECK FOR LEAKS.

SELF-SERVICING

WHEN MAKING A SLOW-RUNNING ADJUSTMENT TO A CARBURETTOR (FIXED JET TYPE SUCH AS A *SOLEX, WEBER* OR *ZENITH*) –

FIRST
1. MAKE SURE THE ROCKER CLEARANCES ARE CORRECT.
2. SEE THAT THE POINTS GAP IS CORRECT.
3. MAKE SURE THE AIR CLEANER IS FAIRLY CLEAN .
4. HAVE THE ENGINE AT NORMAL OPERATING TEMPERATURE .

THE ADJUSTMENT IS MADE ON *TWO* SCREWS –

A. SLOW-RUNNING ADJUSTMENT SCREW OR THROTTLE STOP.
B. THE VOLUME CONTROL SCREW. THIS VARIES THE PETROL/AIR MIXTURE DRAWN INTO THE ENGINE WHEN IT IS IDLING .

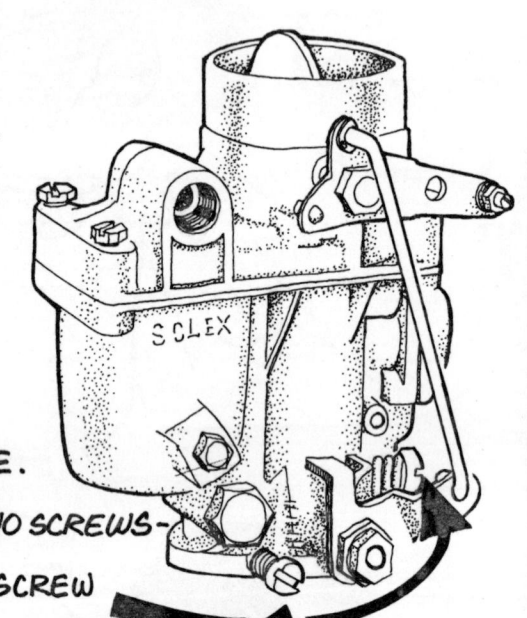

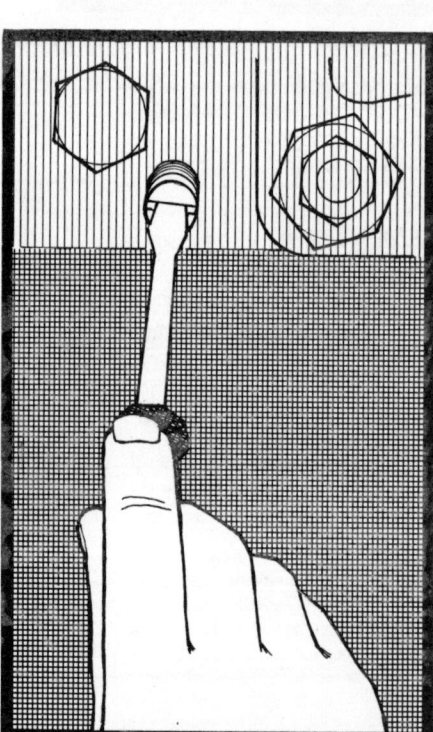

WITH THE ENGINE TICKING OVER –

1 SET THE S.R.A. SCREW (A) TO A FAST IDLE.

2 TURN THE VOLUME SCREW (B) CLOCKWISE UNTIL THE ENGINE SPEED BEGINS TO DROP AND THEN TURN IT BACK ¼ TO ⅓ OF A TURN.

3 READJUST THE S.R.A. SCREW (A) TO GIVE THE BEST IDLING SPEED. DON'T TRY TO GET TOO LOW AN IDLING SPEED.

SELF-SERVICING

SPARKING PLUGS

SIGNS & SYMPTOMS

TROUBLE WITH STARTING, DIFFICULT IDLING, LACK OF POWER AND MISFIRING CAN ALL BE CAUSED BY FAULTY, DIRTY OR WRONGLY SET SPARKING PLUGS.

SO KEEP YOUR PLUGS IN GOOD CONDITION AND BENEFIT FROM BETTER PERFORMANCE AND INCREASED MILEAGE.

TOOLS FOR THE JOB

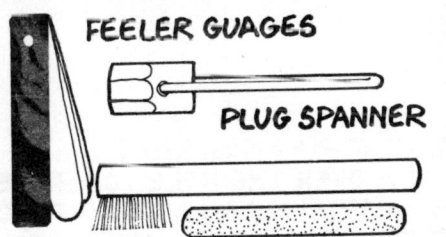

FEELER GUAGES

PLUG SPANNER

PLUG BRUSH & EMERY BOARD

REMOVE THE PLUGS EVERY 5-6,000 MILES. AND BRUSH OFF THE CARBON DEPOSIT. THEN FILE THE POINTS (OR ELECTRODES) TO A BRIGHT METAL SURFACE.

NOW **CHECK** THE **GAP.** FOR MOST CARS IT IS 0·025" (USE FEELER MARKED 25).
TO ALTER THE GAP, BEND THE *OUTER* ELECTRODE ONLY.
RE-FIT PLUGS BUT DO NOT OVERTIGHTEN. THEM.

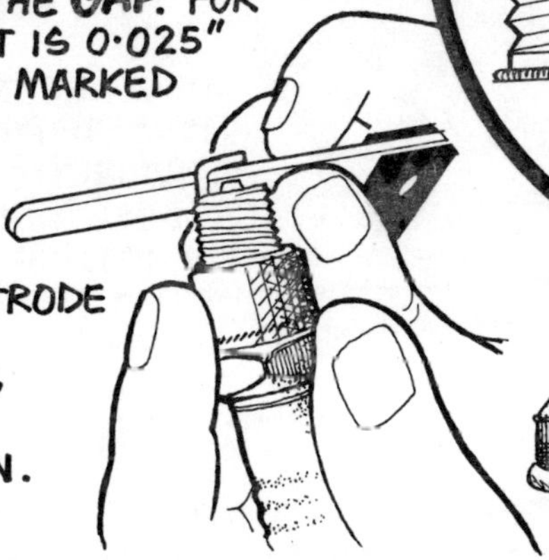

REMEMBER TO FIT NEW PLUGS EVERY 12,000 MILES.

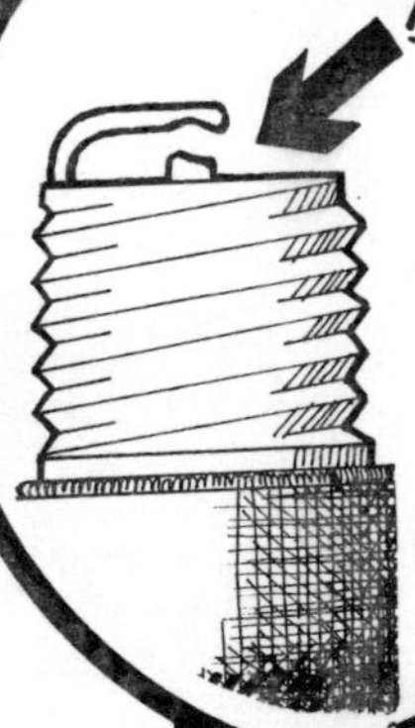

THE GAP TENDS TO INCREASE DUE TO THE BURNING AWAY OF THE POINTS. FILE FLAT AND RESET. OR, IF VERY WORN, THROW AWAY.

CHECK PLUGS FOR...

A *WET BLACK* DEPOSIT WHICH SHOWS A FAULTY PLUG OR A WORN ENGINE.
A *SOFT BLACK* DEPOSIT MEANS THE FUEL MIXTURE IS TOO RICH.
AN *ALMOST WHITE* DEPOSIT MEANS THE MIXTURE IS TOO WEAK.
A *MEDIUM GREY-BROWN* DEPOSIT IS ABOUT RIGHT.

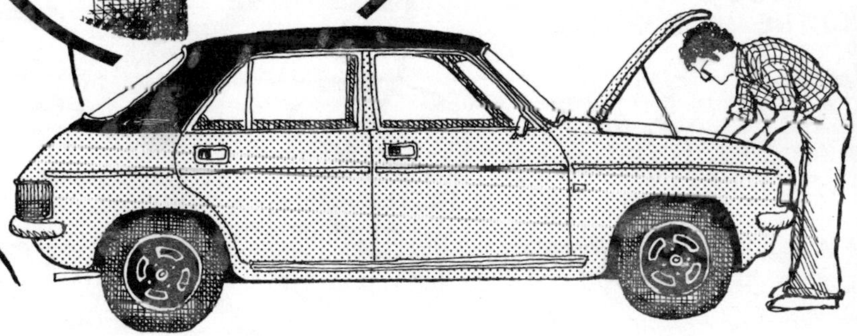

23

SELF-SERVICING

CHECK THE FUEL SUPPLY

IF YOU'RE HAVING TROUBLE STARTING THE CAR AND THE IGNITION SYSTEM AND STARTER HAVE BEEN CHECKED, YOU SHOULD START TO LOOK FOR FUEL FAULTS.
HERE ARE THREE CHECKS TO MAKE ON THE FUEL SYSTEM :—

1 CHECK THAT THE FUEL IS GETTING TO THE CARBURETTOR

2 CHECK FOR BLOCKAGE OR AIR LEAK IN THE FUEL PIPE.

3 TEST PETROL PUMP TO SEE IF IT IS SUCKING.

DISCONNECT THE PIPE FROM THE PUMP TO THE CARBURETTOR AT THE CARBURETTOR END. PUT THE END OF THE PIPE INTO A JAR OF PETROL TURN THE ENGINE OVER BY HAND OR BY USING THE STARTER

IF PETROL SQUIRTS INTO THE JAR, THE PUMP IS WORKING. AN AIR LEAK IN THE FUEL PIPE WILL SHOW AS BUBBLES IN THE PETROL.

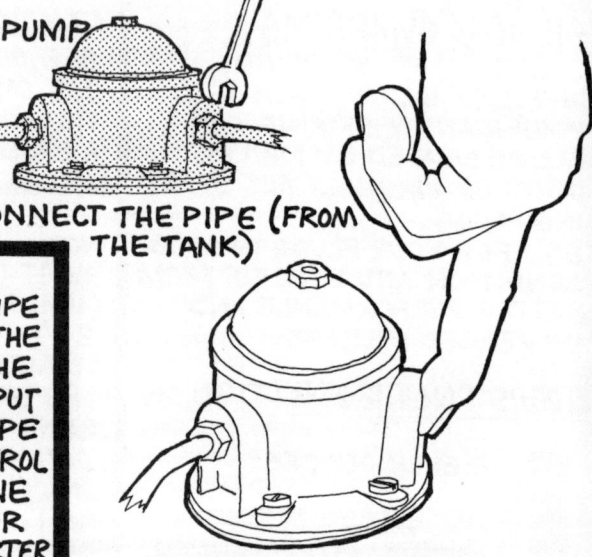

FUEL PUMP

DISCONNECT THE PIPE (FROM THE TANK)

AND PLACE A MOISTENED FINGER OVER THE HOLE. OPERATE THE PUMP AND YOU SHOULD FEEL SUCTION. BLOW DOWN THE PIPE TO CLEAR ANY BLOCKAGE.

SELF~SERVICING

IF YOU ARE HAVING DIFFICULTY STARTING THE CAR AND YOU SUSPECT THE STARTER IS AT FAULT, HERE ARE A FEW CHECKS YOU CAN MAKE ON THE SPOT.

1 STARTER FAILS TO OPERATE .. SWITCH ON THE LIGHTS. IF THE LIGHTS DO NOT COME ON THE BATTERY IS DISCHARGED OR A TERMINAL CONNECTION IS LOOSE.
IF THE LIGHTS ARE WORKING CHECK THE EARTH AND BATTERY LEADS TO THE STARTER.
IF THESE ARE SOUND, THE FAULT LIES IN THE STARTER (TRY A SHARP TAP) OR STARTER SWITCH.

2 IF THE STARTER MAKES A WHIRRING NOISE BUT DOES NOT ENGAGE ... THE BENDIX DRIVE IS NOT WORKING. THIS CAN BE TAKEN OUT AND CLEANED. IT USUALLY WORKS SATISFACTORILY AFTER CLEANING,

3 STARTER TURNS THE ENGINE SLOWLY. VERY LIKELY TO BE A FLAT BATTERY. ALSO CHECK FOR CORRODED BATTERY CABLES LOOSE CONNECTIONS AND BAD ENGINE-TO-CHASSIS EARTH STRAP.

EARTH STRAP

BATTERY

4

STARTER ENGAGES BUT JAMS... PUT THE ENGINE IN TOP GEAR WITH THE IGNITION OFF. ROLL THE CAR BACKWARD AND FORWARDS. IF THIS FAILS, TURN THE STARTER BY THE SQUARED END OF THE SHAFT (UNDER CAP).

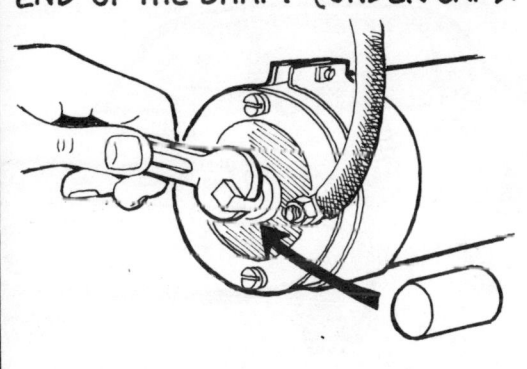

SELF-SERVICING

THE STARTER — CLEAN THE BENDIX DRIVE

IF YOUR STARTER MOTOR MAKES A WHIRRING NOISE BUT DOES NOT ENGAGE, THE STARTER IS TURNING BUT THE *BENDIX* DRIVE IS NOT WORKING. IT IS VERY LIKELY GUMMED UP WITH OIL AND GRIME.
HERE'S HOW TO CLEAN IT (THERE IS NO NEED TO DISMANTLE THE MOTOR)—

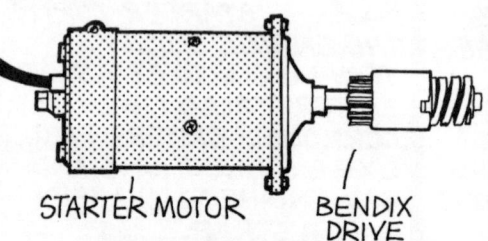

STARTER MOTOR   BENDIX DRIVE

1 DISCONNECT THE POWER LEAD AND UNDO THE BOLTS HOLDING THE STARTER MOTOR TO THE ENGINE FLYWHEEL HOUSING.

2 WASH THE DRIVE THOROUGHLY IN PETROL (DON'T USE OIL GREASE OR PARAFFIN). DO NOT LET IT GET INTO THE MOTOR.

3 OPERATE THE BENDIX — BACK AND FORWARD BY HAND — UNTIL IT IS FREE.

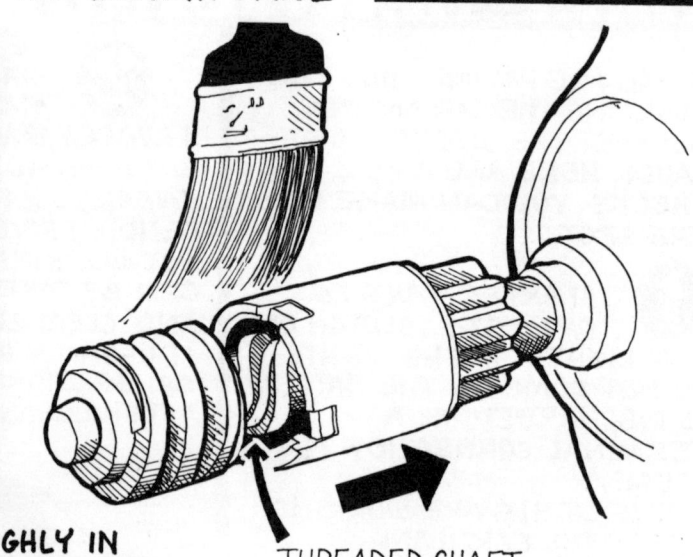

THREADED SHAFT

4 WHEN IT IS DRY, USE A SOFT PENCIL TO PUT A LITTLE DRY GRAPHITE LUBRICANT ON THE THREADED SHAFT.

SELF-SERVICING

FIT NEW HIGH TENSION LEADS

WORN OR BROKEN HIGH TENSION LEADS WILL CAUSE MISFIRING OR STARTING TROUBLE. WHEN FITTING NEW ONES, START BY TAKING THE

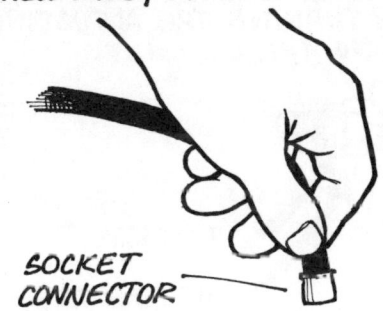

SOCKET CONNECTOR

LONGEST DISTRIBUTOR-TO-SPARK PLUG LEAD, MEASURE IT AND BUY A PIECE OF H.T. CABLE FIVE TIMES ITS LENGTH (7 TIMES FOR SIX CYLINDER ENGINES), SOCKET CONNECTORS AND, IF NECESSARY, NEW SPARK PLUG CAPS.

HIGH TENSION CIRCUIT
COIL-TO DISTRIBUTOR-TO SPARK PLUGS

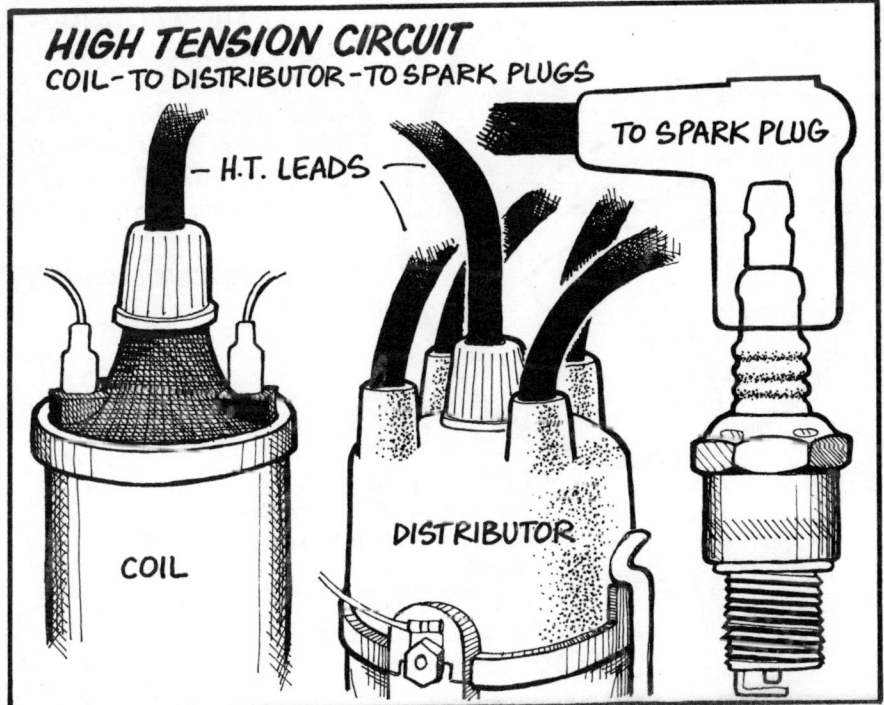

— H.T. LEADS —

TO SPARK PLUG

COIL

DISTRIBUTOR

REPLACE THE LEADS ONE AT A TIME USING THE OLD ONES AS A GUIDE FOR LENGTH.

SCREW THE PLUG CAP ON ONE END AND, WITH PLIERS, CRIMP A SOCKET CONNECTOR ON THE OTHER (TWO SOCKET CONNECTORS ON THE COIL-TO-DISTRIBUTOR LEAD).

THERE ARE TWO TYPES OF H.T. LEAD AVAILABLE — CARBON CORE AND COPPER CORE. BEST STICK TO THE TYPE ORIGINALLY FITTED TO YOUR CAR.

ADJUST CLUTCH PEDAL FREE·PLAY

NORMAL CLUTCH WEAR TENDS TO REDUCE THE FREE PEDAL MOVEMENT SO THAT OCCASIONAL RE-ADJUSTMENT IS REQUIRED.

CLUTCH PEDAL FREE PLAY IS MEASURED AT **A**. CHECK YOUR CAR HANDBOOK FOR THE RECOMMENDED GAP—USUALLY ABOUT 1"

MANY CLUTCHES ARE ADJUSTABLE . THE METHOD VARIES FROM CAR TO CAR (SEE YOUR HANDBOOK) BUT THE SIMPLE ADJUSTMENT MADE BELOW IS TYPICAL OF MOST CABLE AND MANY HYDRAULIC CLUTCHES.
THE LENGTH OF CABLE (OR ROD) OPERATING THE CLUTCH LEVER IS ALTERED IN LENGTH BY TURNING THE ADJUSTING NUT (OR THE ROD) AFTER RELEASING THE LOCKNUT.

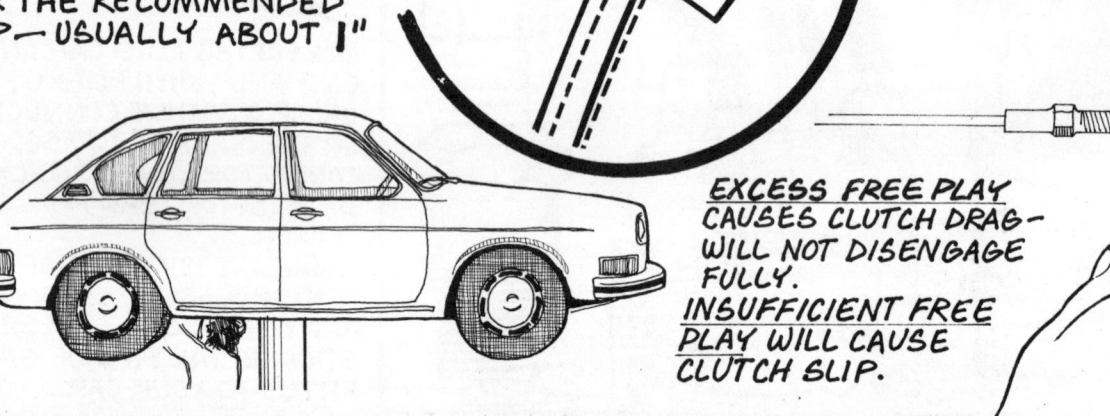

EXCESS FREE PLAY CAUSES CLUTCH DRAG— WILL NOT DISENGAGE FULLY.
INSUFFICIENT FREE PLAY WILL CAUSE CLUTCH SLIP.

LOCKNUT

ADJUSTING NUT

CLUTCH LEVER

SELF-SERVICING

TOP-UP THE REAR AXLE

ONE OF YOUR MAINTENANCE JOBS AT THE 3,000 MILE MARK IS CHECKING THE OIL LEVEL IN THE REAR AXLE. ALSO, IF THE AXLE CAN BE DRAINED, CHANGE THE OIL AT RECOMMENDED INTERVALS (USUALLY 12,000 MILES).

CHECK YOUR HANDBOOK FOR THE CORRECT TYPE OF OIL FOR YOUR CAR. MOST AXLE OILS NOW COME IN PLASTIC SQUEEZE BOTTLES WITH EXTENSION SPOUTS.

LEVEL PLUG

REAR AXLE CASING

THE REAR AXLE LEVEL PLUG IS USUALLY HALF-WAY UP THE SIDE OR THE BACK OF THE CASING

MAKE SURE THE CAR IS LEVEL — TO PREVENT YOU OVER-FILLING OR UNDERFILLING THE BOX. UNDO THE LEVEL PLUG AND INJECT THE OIL UNTIL IT RUNS OUT. BEFORE YOU REPLACE THE PLUG ALLOW THE OIL TO SETTLE OR YOU MAY TRAP EXCESS OIL IN THE BOX.

SELF~SERVICING

WINDSCREEN WIPERS DETERIORATE ALMOST UNNOTICED, SO THAT YOU'RE DRIVING IN THE WET WITH POOR VISIBILITY UNAWARE OF HOW LITTLE YOU CAN

REALLY SEE. PLAY SAFE AND KEEP YOUR WIPERS IN GOOD ORDER. SUMMER AND WINTER.

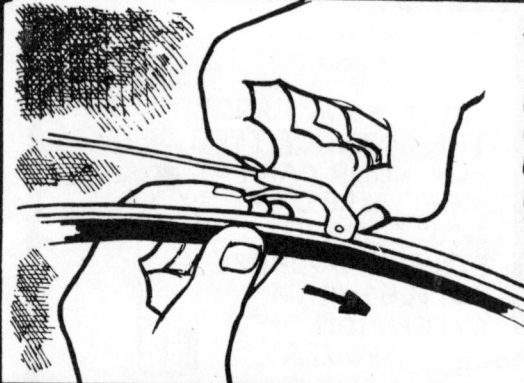

THE RUBBERS ON WIPERS DON'T GIVE A PERFECT WIPE FOR LONG. SO ITS USUALLY RECOMMENDED THAT YOU CHANGE THE COMPLETE BLADES AT LEAST ONCE A YEAR (REPLACEMENT RUBBERS ARE ONLY AVAILABLE FOR A VERY FEW CARS NOW).

FITTING IS EASY - RELEASE THE SPRING CLIP, SLIDE OLD ONE OFF AND SLIDE THE NEW ONE ON AND LET IT CLICK INTO POSITION.

THE WIPER ARM NEEDS REPLACING ALMOST AS FREQUENTLY. IT MAY LOOK SOUND BUT THE SPRING HOLDING IT AGAINST THE SCREEN BECOMES WEAK AND ALLOWS THE ARM TO 'LIFT'.

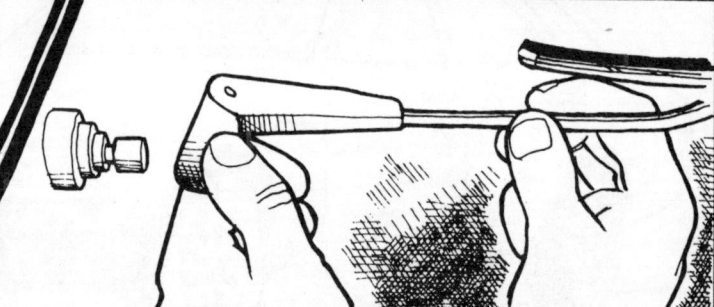

FITTING A NEW CONDENSER

A DEFECTIVE CONDENSER (OR CAPACITOR) CAN CAUSE STARTING TROUBLE, MISFIRING OR FAILURE OF THE IGNITION SYSTEM BY BURNING OUT CONTACT BREAKER POINTS.

ONE CLUE THAT YOUR CONDENSER IS THE OFFENDER (AND NOT FAULTY PLUGS OR LEADS ETC.) IS A SLIGHT BLUEY APPEARANCE OF POINTS SURFACES.

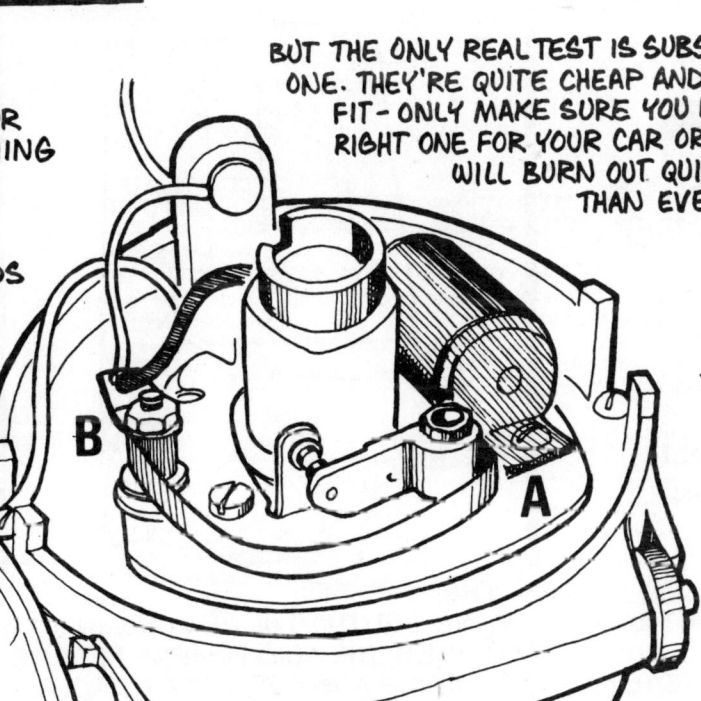

UNCLIP THE DISTRIBUTOR CAP AND LIFT OFF THE ROTOR ARM TO GET AT THE CONDENSER

BUT THE ONLY REAL TEST IS SUBSTITUTING A NEW ONE. THEY'RE QUITE CHEAP AND EASY TO FIT - ONLY MAKE SURE YOU HAVE THE RIGHT ONE FOR YOUR CAR OR YOUR POINTS WILL BURN OUT QUICKER THAN EVER.

UNDO THE SCREW "A" HOLDING THE SMALL BRACKET TO THE BASE PLATE OF THE DISTRIBUTOR. REMOVE THE NUT AND WASHER "B" WITH THE CONDENSER LEAD TAG AND LIFT THE CONDENSER OUT. FIT THE NEW ONE IN REVERSE ORDER.

SELF~SERVICING

PREVENT BATTERY CORROSION

NEXT TIME YOU CLEAN YOUR BATTERY, TAKE

THESE STEPS TO PREVENT CORROSION
RECURRING —

BRUSH OFF THE WHITE DEPOSIT. THEN WASH DOWN THE
BATTERY, TRAY AND SECURING STRAP WITH A STRONG SOLUTION OF AMMONIA IN WARM
WATER (KEEP IT AWAY FROM THE EYES). THIS NEUTRALISES THE ACID FUMES. BEFORE RE-
CONNECTING THE BATTERY, SMEAR THE TERMINALS, INSIDE AND OUT, WITH PETROLEUM JELLY.

MOST IMPORTANT OF ALL - ALWAYS
KEEP THE FILLER CAPS OR LID FIRMLY IN
POSITION TO STOP
ACID FUMES
LEAKING OUT.

SELF~SERVICING

LUBRICATE HINGES ETC.

IT'S EASY TO FORGET SMALL ITEMS IN THE MAINTENANCE SCHEDULE

USING MACHINE OIL, LUBRICATE DOOR HINGES, LOCKS, BONNET AND BOOT HINGES AND SEAT RUNNERS. ALSO PUT A SMALL DAB OF GREASE ON THE DOOR-LOCK STRIKER PLATE

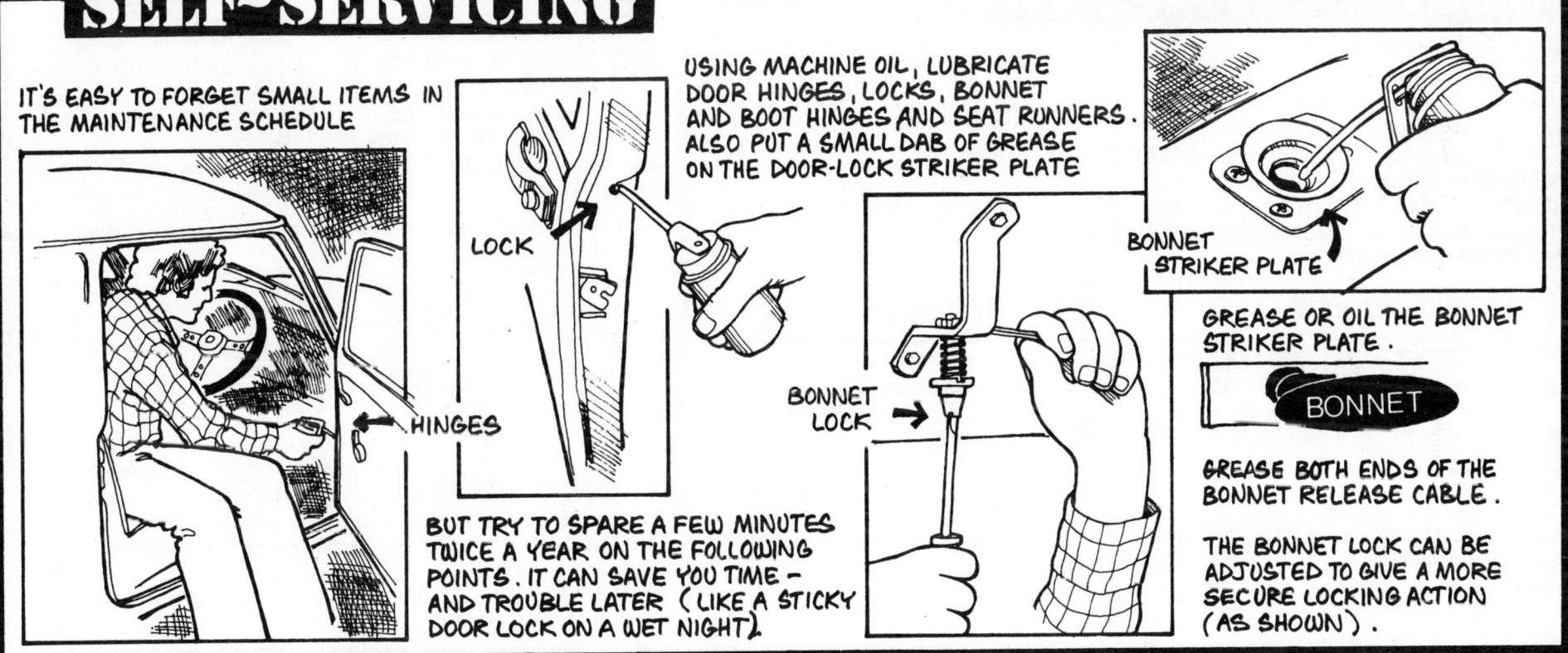

LOCK

HINGES

BONNET STRIKER PLATE

BONNET LOCK

BONNET

BUT TRY TO SPARE A FEW MINUTES TWICE A YEAR ON THE FOLLOWING POINTS. IT CAN SAVE YOU TIME — AND TROUBLE LATER (LIKE A STICKY DOOR LOCK ON A WET NIGHT).

GREASE OR OIL THE BONNET STRIKER PLATE.

GREASE BOTH ENDS OF THE BONNET RELEASE CABLE.

THE BONNET LOCK CAN BE ADJUSTED TO GIVE A MORE SECURE LOCKING ACTION (AS SHOWN).

33

SELF-SERVICING

HOW TO FIT A NEW FAN BELT

SIGNS & SYMPTOMS

WHEN THE FAN BELT BREAKS, THE RED WARNING LIGHT ON THE DASHBOARD GLOWS BRIGHTLY. THIS MEANS:
① THE ENGINE WILL VERY QUICKLY START OVERHEATING; ② NO ELECTRIC CURRENT FROM THE DYNAMO SO THAT THE CAR IS NOW POWERED, ELECTRICALLY, ONLY FROM THE BATTERY.

TOOLS FOR THE JOB

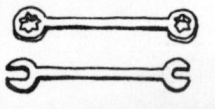 

TWO SPANNERS

A PIECE OF WOOD FOR A LEVER

MATERIALS

A FAN BELT OF CORRECT SIZE FOR YOUR CAR. SEE YOUR HANDBOOK OR ASK AT A GARAGE – GIVE YOUR CAR'S MAKE, MODEL & YEAR.

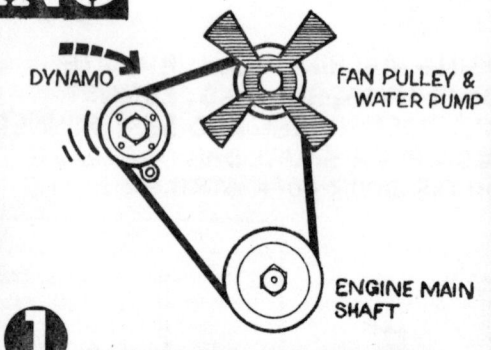

DYNAMO

FAN PULLEY & WATER PUMP

ENGINE MAIN SHAFT

① TO REMOVE THE OLD BELT, THE DYNAMO MUST BE MOVED INWARDS ON ITS PIVOT.

② THIS IS DONE BY LOOSENING CLAMP NUTS ① AND, IF NECESSARY, PIVOT NUTS ② & ③

③ TAKE THE NEW BELT AND CHECK CAREFULLY FOR FAULTS THEN PLACE IT IN POSITION OVER THE FAN AND ROUND ALL THREE PULLEYS.

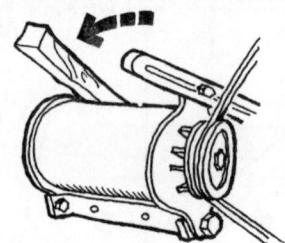

3/4"

④ LEVER THE DYNAMO AWAY FROM THE ENGINE AND TIGHTEN NUTS. CORRECT TENSION OF THE BELT IS FOUND WHEN THERE IS ABOUT 3/4" PLAY IN THE MIDDLE OF THE LONGEST SIDE.
ON SOME CARS THE PIVOT MAY BE ON TOP WITH THE CLAMP BOLTS UNDERNEATH.

SELF-SERVICING

BLEED THE BRAKES

SIGNS & SYMPTOMS

IF THE BRAKES FEEL 'SPONGY' THERE COULD BE AIR IN THE BRAKE FLUID. WE REMOVE THE AIR (WHICH REDUCES EFFICIENCY) BY 'BLEEDING' THE SYSTEM.

TOOLS FOR THE JOB

A SPANNER TO FIT THE BLEED NIPPLE

A FOOT OF THIN RUBBER TUBING

A CLEAN JAR, AND AN ASSISTANT

MATERIALS

AN 8oz CAN OF BRAKE FLUID OF THE CORRECT TYPE & GRADE FOR YOUR CAR (SEE HANDBOOK).

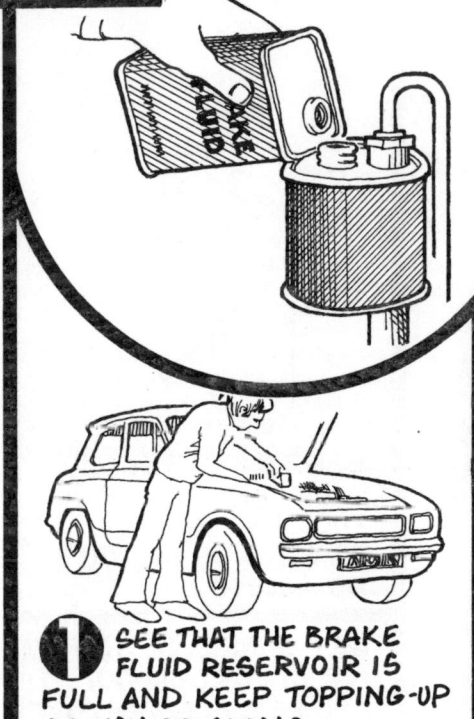

1 SEE THAT THE BRAKE FLUID RESERVOIR IS FULL AND KEEP TOPPING-UP AS YOU GO ALONG.

2 FIND THE BLEED NIPPLE AND SLIP THE RING SPANNER OVER IT. FIT THE TUBING TO THE BLEED SCREW AND PUT THE OTHER END IN THE JAR OF FLUID. OPEN THE BLEED SCREW.

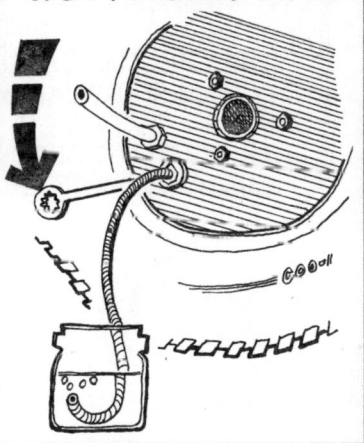

3 THEN GET YOUR PARTNER TO DEPRESS THE BRAKE PEDAL QUICKLY FOR A FULL STROKE AND ALLOW IT TO RETURN SLOWLY. THEN REPEAT A FEW TIMES. AIR BUBBLES WILL STREAM FROM THE IMMERSED END OF THE TUBE.

4 WHEN AIR BUBBLES NO LONGER COME OUT, ASK YOUR HELPER TO HOLD THE PEDAL DOWN AT THE END OF A FULL STROKE WHILE YOU TIGHTEN THE BLEED SCREW. REPEAT WITH THE OTHER THREE BRAKES AND MAKE A FINAL CHECK ON THE FLUID RESERVOIR.

# SELF~SERVICING

HOW TO BLEED THE CLUTCH

IN HYDRAULICALLY OPERATED CLUTCHES, AIR IN THE SYSTEM WILL CAUSE EXCESSIVE PEDAL MOVEMENT.
THE CURE IS TO BLEED THE SYSTEM.
THIS IS DONE IN THE SAME WAY AS FOR HYDRAULIC BRAKES.

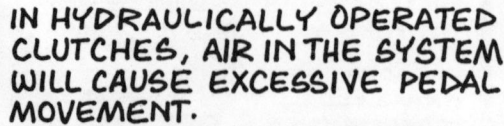

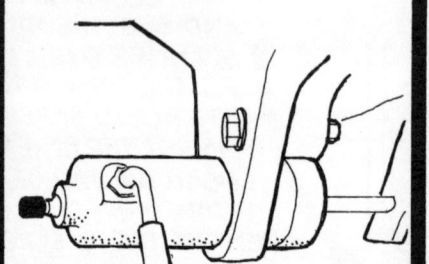

FIND THE CLUTCH SLAVE CYLINDER - USUALLY BOLTED TO THE SIDE OF THE CLUTCH HOUSING AT SUMP HEIGHT.

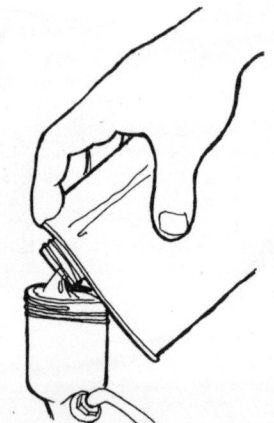

SEE THAT THE CLUTCH FLUID RESERVOIR IS FULL AND KEEP TOPPING UP AS YOU GO ALONG.

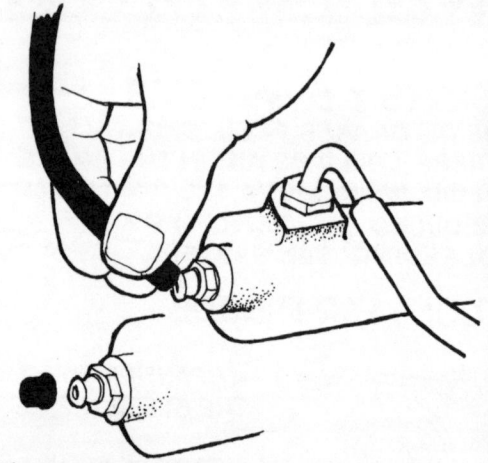

TAKE THE DUST COVER OFF THE BLEED NIPPLE AND FIT A LENGTH OF RUBBER TUBING TO IT WITH THE OTHER END IN A JAR OF FLUID.
OPEN THE BLEED SCREW.

GET SOMEONE TO PUMP THE CLUTCH PEDAL UNTIL THE AIR IS FORCED OUT. TIGHTEN NIPPLE, TAKE OFF TUBING AND REPLACE THE COVER. CHECK THE CLUTCH ACTION.

SELF-SERVICING

THE AIR FILTER

THE AIR FILTER SHOULD BE REPLACED OR CLEANED EVERY 12,000 MILES. FOR THE PAPER TYPE, SIMPLY LIFT OUT THE ELEMENT AND DROP IN A REPLACEMENT.

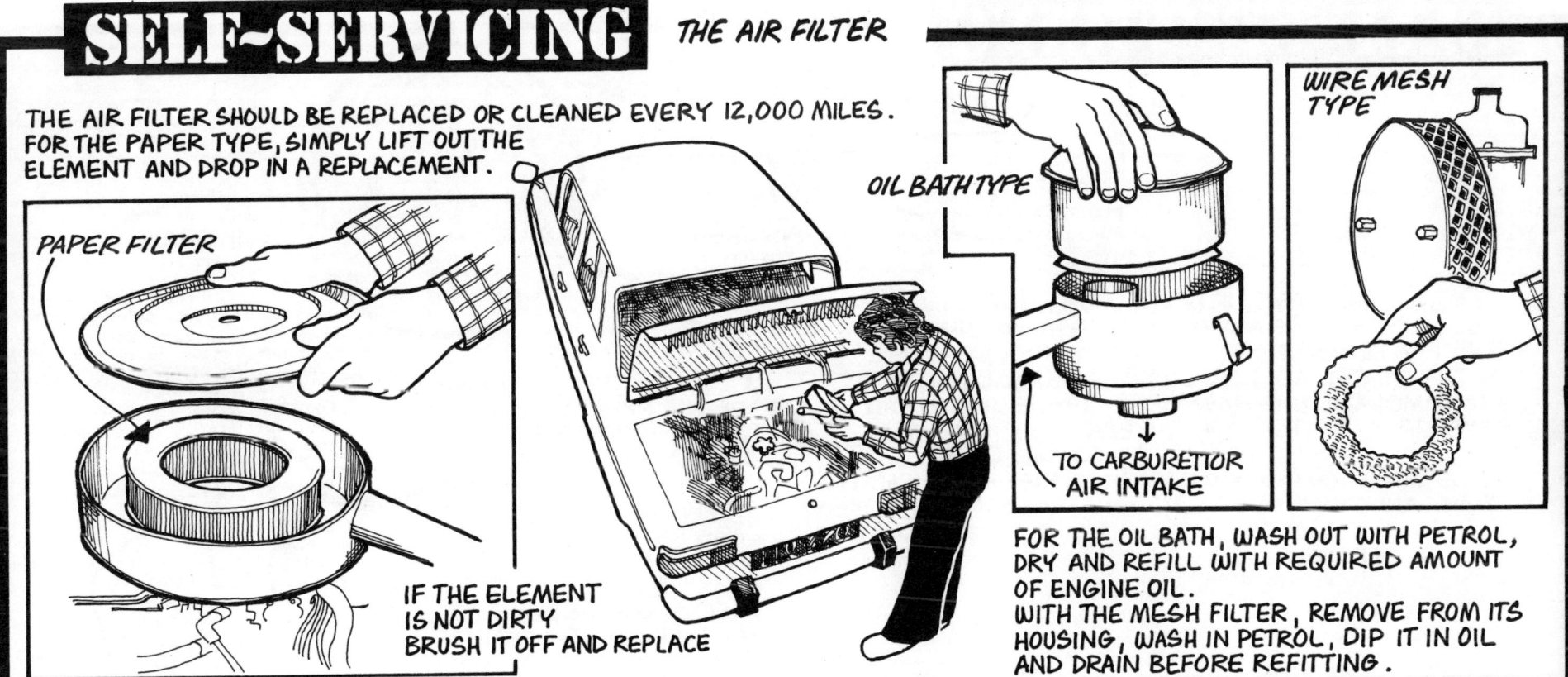

PAPER FILTER

IF THE ELEMENT IS NOT DIRTY BRUSH IT OFF AND REPLACE

OIL BATH TYPE

TO CARBURETTOR AIR INTAKE

WIRE MESH TYPE

FOR THE OIL BATH, WASH OUT WITH PETROL, DRY AND REFILL WITH REQUIRED AMOUNT OF ENGINE OIL.
WITH THE MESH FILTER, REMOVE FROM ITS HOUSING, WASH IN PETROL, DIP IT IN OIL AND DRAIN BEFORE REFITTING.

SELF~SERVICING

CHECKING THE DRIVE SHAFT

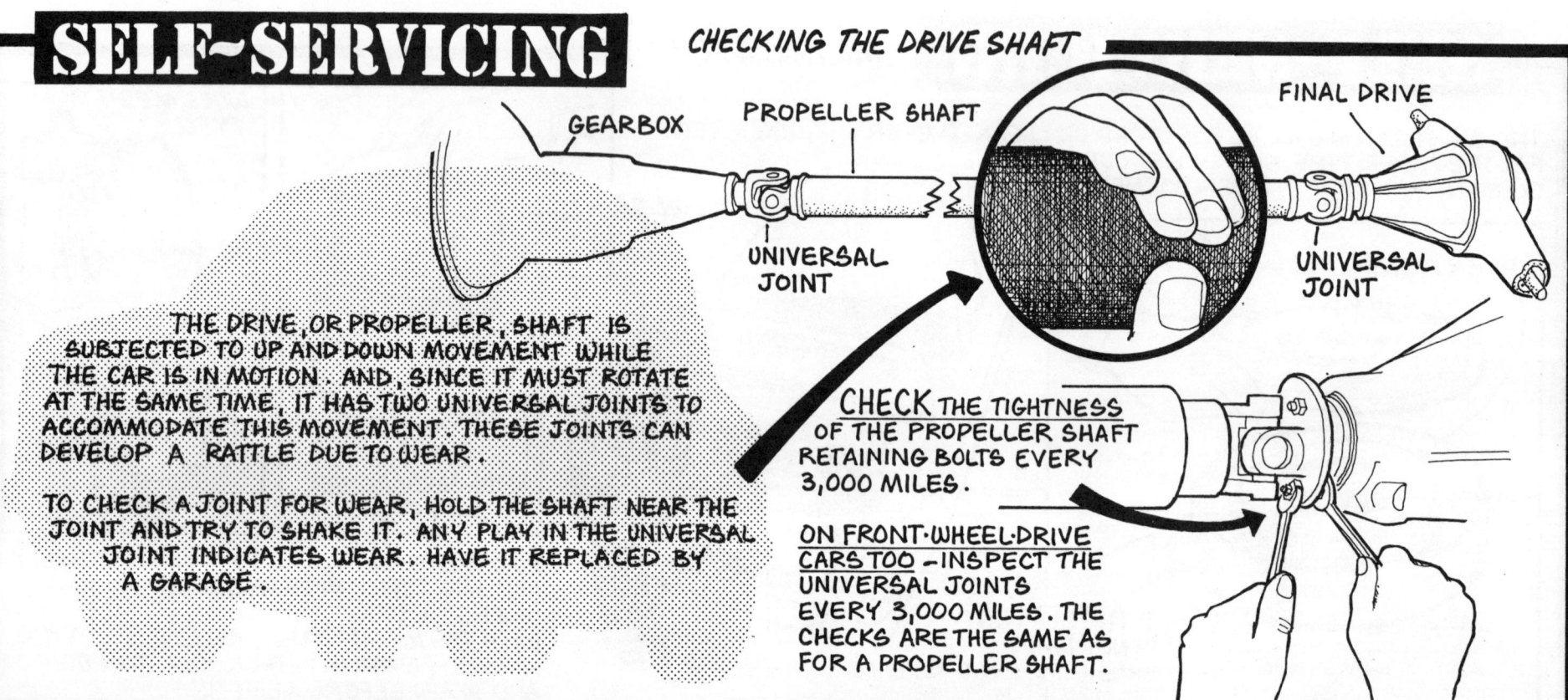

GEARBOX

PROPELLER SHAFT

FINAL DRIVE

UNIVERSAL JOINT

UNIVERSAL JOINT

THE DRIVE, OR PROPELLER, SHAFT IS SUBJECTED TO UP AND DOWN MOVEMENT WHILE THE CAR IS IN MOTION. AND, SINCE IT MUST ROTATE AT THE SAME TIME, IT HAS TWO UNIVERSAL JOINTS TO ACCOMMODATE THIS MOVEMENT. THESE JOINTS CAN DEVELOP A RATTLE DUE TO WEAR.

TO CHECK A JOINT FOR WEAR, HOLD THE SHAFT NEAR THE JOINT AND TRY TO SHAKE IT. ANY PLAY IN THE UNIVERSAL JOINT INDICATES WEAR. HAVE IT REPLACED BY A GARAGE.

CHECK THE TIGHTNESS OF THE PROPELLER SHAFT RETAINING BOLTS EVERY 3,000 MILES.

ON FRONT·WHEEL·DRIVE CARS TOO — INSPECT THE UNIVERSAL JOINTS EVERY 3,000 MILES. THE CHECKS ARE THE SAME AS FOR A PROPELLER SHAFT.

SELF~SERVICING

CHECK AND SERVICE THE DYNAMO I

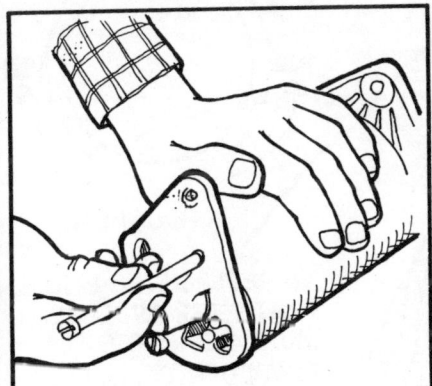

REMOVE THE DYNAMO FROM THE CAR (FOR MOST CARS DISCONNECT THE LEADS, SLACKEN MOUNTING BOLTS AND TAKE OFF FAN BELT. THEN REMOVE THE MOUNTING BOLTS AND LIFT OFF THE DYNAMO.)
CLEAN THE DYNAMO THEN TAKE OUT THE TWO THROUGH BOLTS.

THEN THE COMMUTATOR END-BRACKET COMPLETE WITH BRUSH GEAR CAN BE PULLED OFF.

PULL THE ARMATURE ASSEMBLY OUT OF THE BODY.
NOW CLEAN THE COMMUTATOR (THE SEGMENTED COPPER CYLINDER). IT SHOULD BE CLEAN AND SMOOTH AND THE INSULATION BETWEEN THE SEGMENTS 'GROOVED'.
IF THE COMMUTATOR IS DISCOLOURED, CLEAN IT WITH A FUEL-MOISTENED CLOTH. AND, IF NECESSARY, WRAP A PIECE OF VERY FINE GLASSPAPER ROUND IT AND RUB WITH A TWISTING ACTION (CLEAN AWAY ALL DUST).
FINALLY, USE A PIN TO CLEAN THE GROOVES BETWEEN THE SEGMENTS OF THE COMMUTATOR.

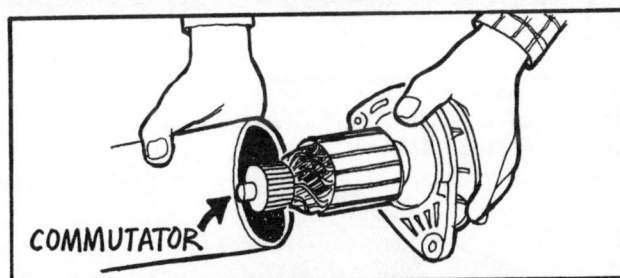

COMMUTATOR

GROOVES

CHECK AND SERVICE THE DYNAMO II

AFTER CLEANING THE COMMUTATOR, THE ARMATURE ASSEMBLY CAN BE REPLACED IN THE BODY OF THE DYNAMO.

COMMUTATOR END-PLATE

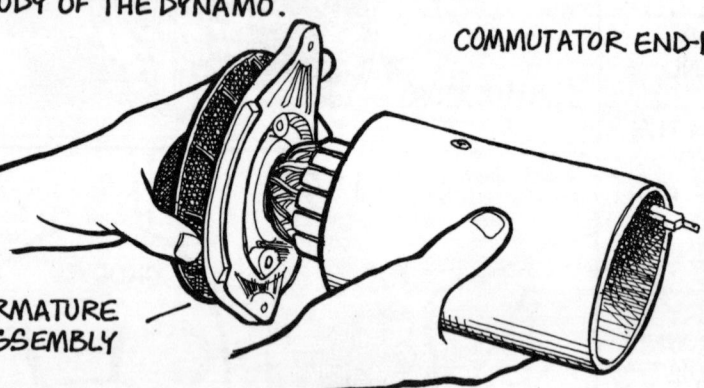

ARMATURE ASSEMBLY

COMMUTATOR

BRUSHES

BRUSHES

THEN TAKE THE COMMUTATOR END-PLATE (WHICH HOLDS THE BRUSH GEAR) AND CHECK THE BRUSHES. IT IS USUALLY BETTER TO FIT A NEW SET WHETHER THEY ARE BADLY WORN OR NOT. *JUST UNSCREW* THE TERMINAL TAG AND PULL THE BRUSH AND ITS CONNECTING WIRE FROM THE

GUIDE. CLEAN THE GUIDE AND CHECK THE SPRING. IF IN DOUBT, FIT A NEW ONE. *WITH THE NEW BRUSH IN POSITION*, MAKE SURE THAT IT SLIDES FREELY IN ITS GUIDE. THEN FIT THE SECOND ONE.

TO REPLACE THE END-PLATE, THE BRUSHES MUST CLEAR THE COMMUTATOR. LIFT BOTH SPRINGS AND HOOK THEM OVER THE GUIDES.

FIT THE END-PLATE, WITH BOLTS, THEN PUSH A SCREWDRIVER THROUGH THE END-PLATE HOLE. AND *FIX THE SPRINGS* SO THAT THEY AGAIN PRESS ON THE BRUSHES.

SELF~SERVICING

TOOLS FOR THE JOB
ELECTRIC DRILL WITH SANDING DISC; HAMMER;
FILLER PASTE AND CATALYST; A SHEET OF PERFORATED ZINC;
WET·AND·DRY PAPER (GRADES 80, 240 & 400) AND A SANDING BLOCK

1

2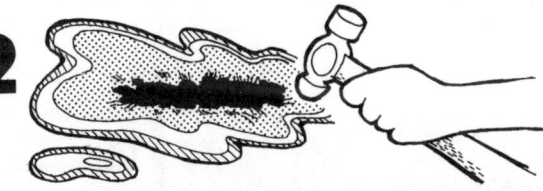

1 SAND DOWN TO THE BARE METAL FOR A FEW INCHES AROUND THE ROTTEN AREA.

2 HAMMER THE EDGES OF THE HOLE SO YOU HAVE A DEPRESSION TO FILL.

3 MIX THE FILLER AND APPLY IT IN LAYERS TO BRING THE SURFACE PROUD OF THE METALWORK (IF THE HOLE IS LARGE, USE A SHEET OF ZINC BEHIND IT TO SUPPORT THE FILLER).

4 WHEN THE FILLER IS HARD, RUB DOWN WITH PROGRESSIVELY FINER GRADES OF WET-AND-DRY PAPER (USE PLENTY OF WATER). ALLOW IT TO DRY BEFORE PAINTING.

3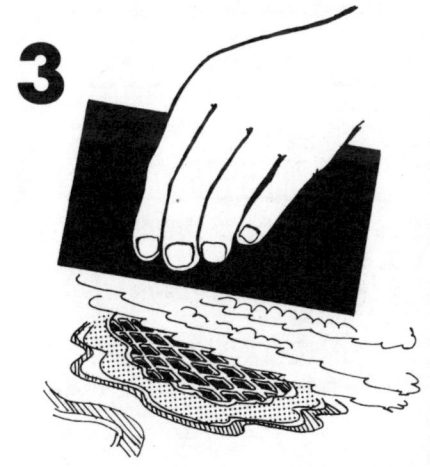

4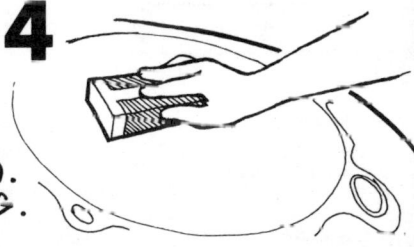

41

TOOLS FOR THE JOB

COARSE FILE

SOFT-HEADED HAMMER OR SIMILAR

WET-AND-DRY PAPER GRADES 80, 240 & 400

SANDING BLOCK

FILLER & CATALYST

FILLER   HARDENER

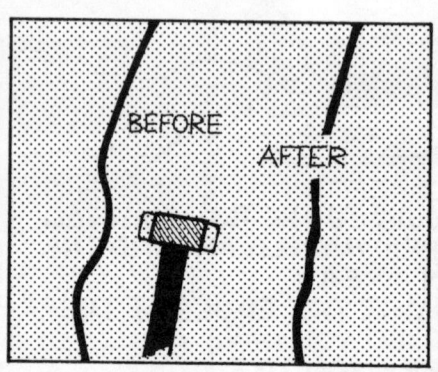

BEFORE   AFTER

PUSH OUT OR BEAT OUT LARGE DENTS.
RUB DOWN TO BARE METAL WITH COARSE (80 GRADE) WET-AND-DRY PAPER.

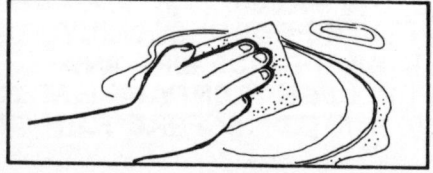

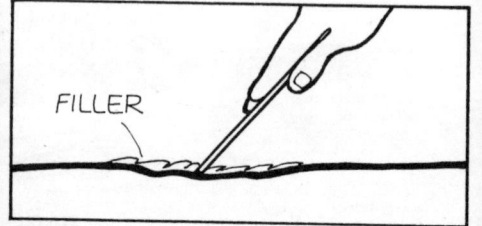

FILLER

MIX THE FILLER PASTE AND APPLY IT QUICKLY. YOU MAY NEED SEVERAL APPLICATIONS (ALLOW TO DRY BETWEEN EACH ONE) TO BRING THE SURFACE SLIGHTLY ABOVE THE SURROUNDING BODYWORK.

WHEN THE FILLER IS HARD, ROUGH-SHAPE IT WITH A COARSE FILE.

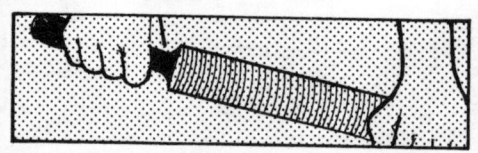

NOW RUB DOWN WITH WET-AND-DRY PAPER USING PLENTY OF WATER AND FINER GRADES AS THE FILLER BLENDS TO THE SHAPE OF THE CAR BODY.

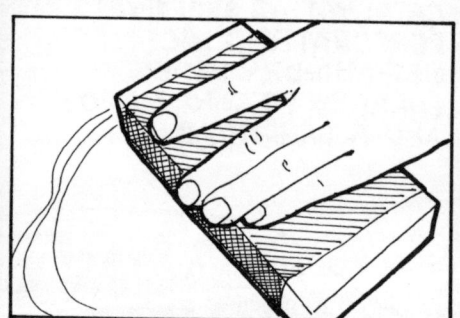

FILL ANY AIR HOLES OR SCRATCHES WITH FILLER AND REPEAT THE SMOOTHING-DOWN PROCESS. ALLOW IT TO DRY BEFORE PAINTING.

SELF~SERVICING

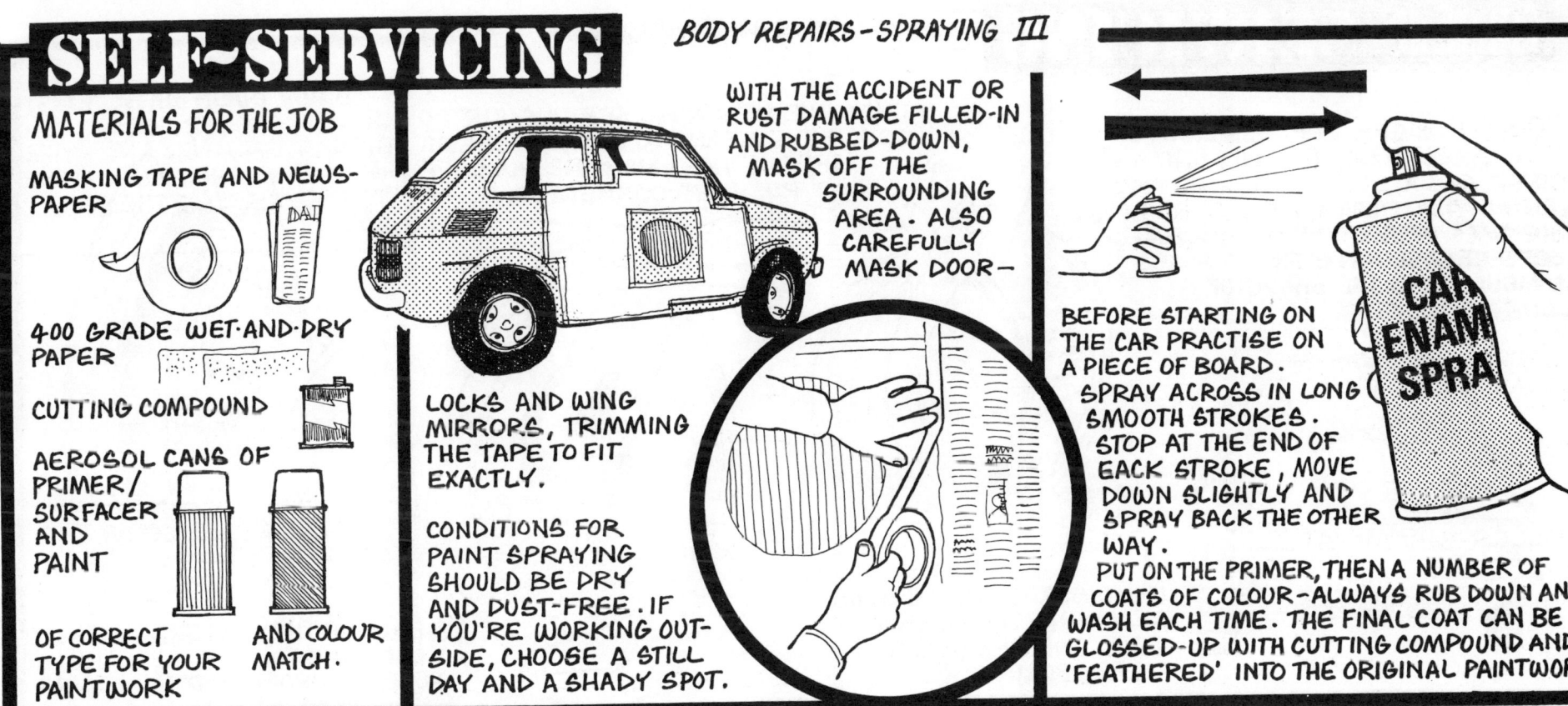

MATERIALS FOR THE JOB

MASKING TAPE AND NEWS-PAPER

4.00 GRADE WET-AND-DRY PAPER

CUTTING COMPOUND

AEROSOL CANS OF PRIMER/SURFACER AND PAINT

OF CORRECT TYPE FOR YOUR PAINTWORK

AND COLOUR MATCH.

WITH THE ACCIDENT OR RUST DAMAGE FILLED-IN AND RUBBED-DOWN, MASK OFF THE SURROUNDING AREA. ALSO CAREFULLY MASK DOOR-

LOCKS AND WING MIRRORS, TRIMMING THE TAPE TO FIT EXACTLY.

CONDITIONS FOR PAINT SPRAYING SHOULD BE DRY AND DUST-FREE. IF YOU'RE WORKING OUT-SIDE, CHOOSE A STILL DAY AND A SHADY SPOT.

CAR ENAM SPRA

BEFORE STARTING ON THE CAR PRACTISE ON A PIECE OF BOARD. SPRAY ACROSS IN LONG SMOOTH STROKES. STOP AT THE END OF EACK STROKE, MOVE DOWN SLIGHTLY AND SPRAY BACK THE OTHER WAY.

PUT ON THE PRIMER, THEN A NUMBER OF COATS OF COLOUR—ALWAYS RUB DOWN AND WASH EACH TIME. THE FINAL COAT CAN BE GLOSSED-UP WITH CUTTING COMPOUND AND 'FEATHERED' INTO THE ORIGINAL PAINTWORK.

SELF~SERVICING

FITTING A NEW HEADLAMP

MOST MODERN CAR HEADLIGHTS HAVE *SEALED BEAM* LIGHT UNITS. THESE ARE ALL GLASS, SEALED AND CONTAIN TWO FILAMENTS BUT NO BULB. THE BACK OF THE UNIT IS A SILVERED REFLECTOR AND THE FRONT GLASS IS MOULDED IN THE SHAPE OF A LENS.

1 UNDO SCREW OR SCREWS RETAINING THE HEADLIGHT TRIM AND REMOVE IT CAREFULLY.

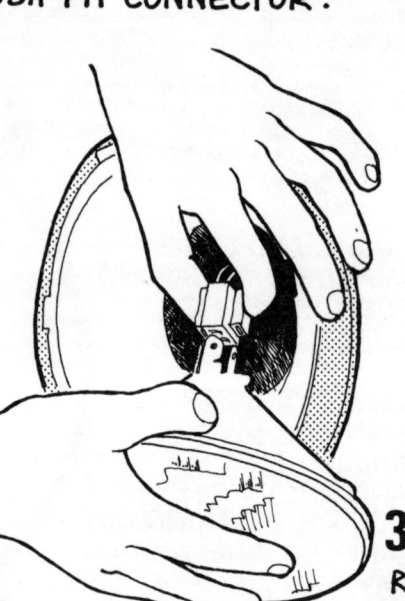

2 UNDO THE RETAINING SCREWS BUT DO NOT TOUCH THE BEAM ADJUSTING SCREWS. THEN LIFT OUT THE LAMP AND PULL OFF THE PUSH-FIT CONNECTOR.

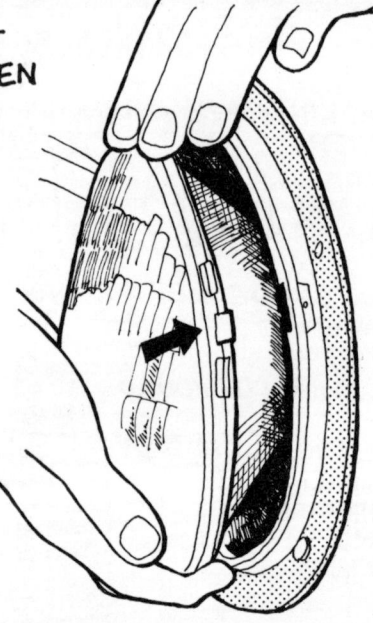

3 LINE UP THE NEW UNIT BY THE LOCATING TAB AND REFIT IN REVERSE ORDER TO DISMANTLING.

SELF-SERVICING

MAKE SURE THE TYRE PRESSURES ARE CORRECT AND HAVE THE REAR SEAT WEIGHTED WITH ONE PASSENGER. WITH THE CAR ON LEVEL GROUND AND AGAINST A WALL, CHALK A CROSS TO MARK THE POSITION OF EACH HEADLAMP.

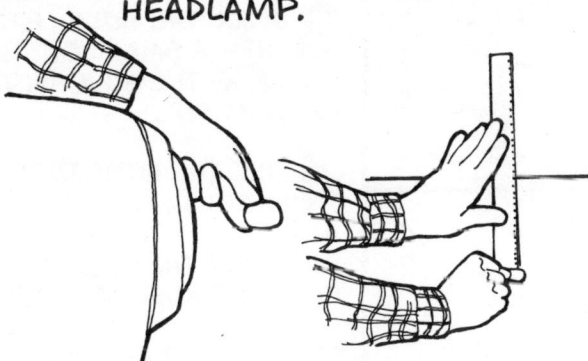

REVERSE THE CAR 25 FEET FROM THE WALL AND SWITCH ON THE HEADLIGHTS (MAIN BEAM). THE BRIGHTEST AREAS SHOULD BE JUST BELOW EACH CROSS.

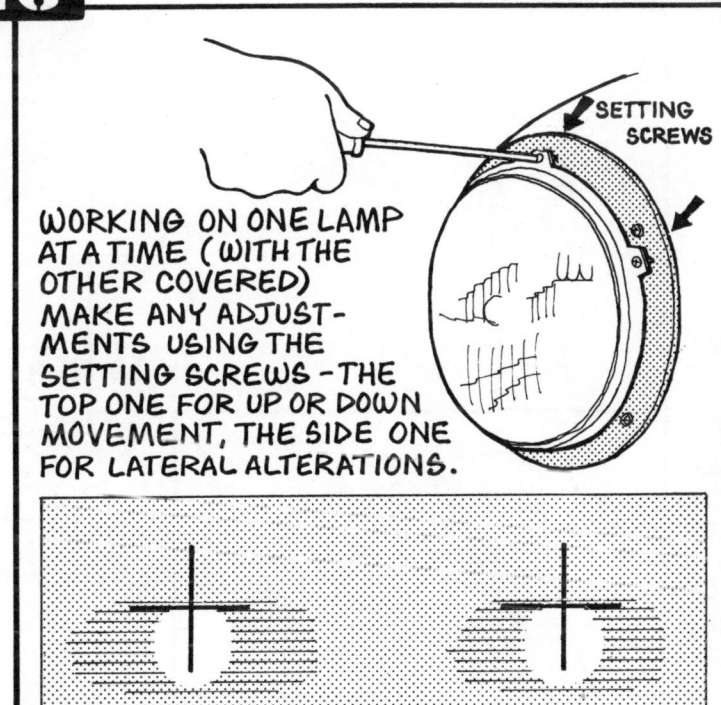

SETTING SCREWS

WORKING ON ONE LAMP AT A TIME (WITH THE OTHER COVERED) MAKE ANY ADJUSTMENTS USING THE SETTING SCREWS – THE TOP ONE FOR UP OR DOWN MOVEMENT, THE SIDE ONE FOR LATERAL ALTERATIONS.

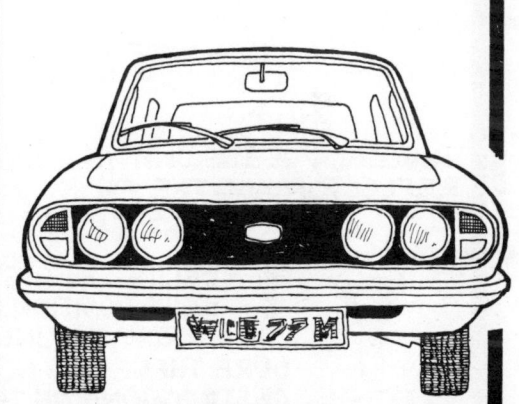

ON 4-HEADLAMP CARS, TWO OF THE LAMPS (OUTER) SUPPLY MAINLY DIPPED BEAM – THEY MUST BE SET ON DIPPED BEAM. SO WHEN REPLACING A DIP LAMP, LINE IT UP USING THE OTHER ONE AS A GUIDE. THEN HAVE IT SET AT A GARAGE.

FITTING WING MIRRORS

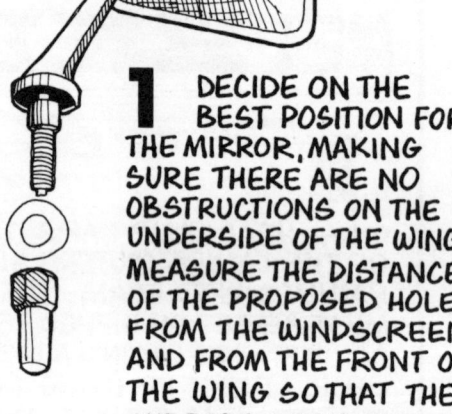

1 DECIDE ON THE BEST POSITION FOR THE MIRROR, MAKING SURE THERE ARE NO OBSTRUCTIONS ON THE UNDERSIDE OF THE WING. MEASURE THE DISTANCE OF THE PROPOSED HOLE FROM THE WINDSCREEN AND FROM THE FRONT OF THE WING SO THAT THE MIRRORS GET FITTED IN THE SAME POSITION ON BOTH SIDES.

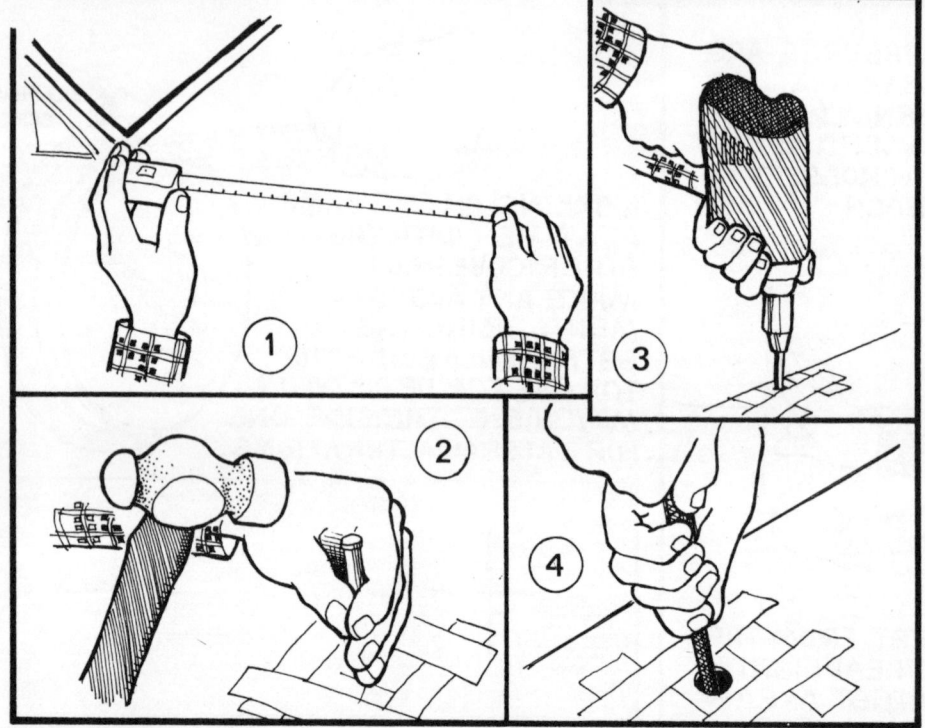

2 MARK THE SPOT AND MAKE A START FOR THE DRILL USING A CENTRE PUNCH. STICK MASKING TAPE ROUND THE MARK TO PREVENT THE DRILL POINT SLIPPING.

3 DRILL THE HOLE, FIRST WITH A SMALL BIT, THEN ENLARGE THE HOLE WITH A LARGER BIT.

4 FILE THE HOLE TO THE EXACT SIZE REQUIRED. AND PAINT PRIMER ON THE EDGES OF THE HOLE TO PREVENT RUST STARTING.

FIT THE MIRROR, USING A BOX SPANNER TO TIGHTEN THE RETAINING NUT UNDER THE WING.

SELF~SERVICING

THE ELECTRICAL COMPONENTS IN A CAR (HEADLAMPS, HORN ETC) ARE CONNECTED THROUGH SWITCHES TO THE POSITIVE BATTERY TERMINAL . THE OTHER TERMINAL IS CONNECTED TO THE CAR BODY OR CHASSIS. IN THIS WAY THE CIRCUIT TO ANY COMPONENT IS COMPLETED THROUGH THE BODY OF THE CAR .

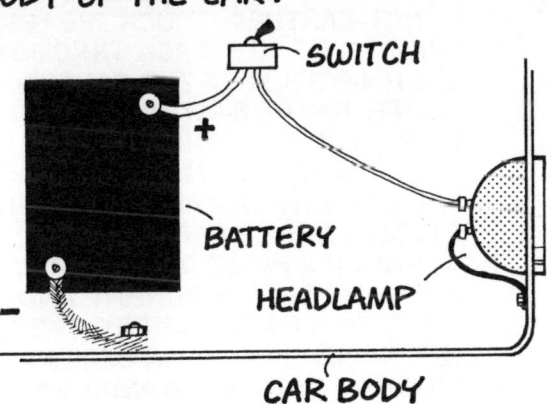

SWITCH

+

BATTERY

HEADLAMP

-

CAR BODY

USING A CIRCUIT-TESTING LAMP WE CAN TRACE THE CURRENT FROM POINT TO POINT IN A CIRCUIT SO THAT A BREAK CAN BE LOCATED .

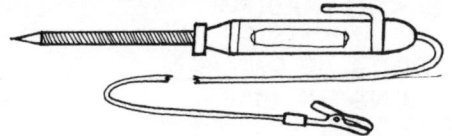

SWITCH ON IGNITION AND ATTACH THE LEAD FROM THE TESTER TO THE CAR BODY (EARTH) AND THE PROBE END TO THE COMPONENTS POWER SUPPLY. CHECK BACK AT EACH JOINT AND CONNECTION IN THE WIRING UNTIL THE TEST BULB LIGHTS . ANY FAULT IN THE SUPPLY CAN BE ISOLATED IN THIS WAY AND REPAIRED .

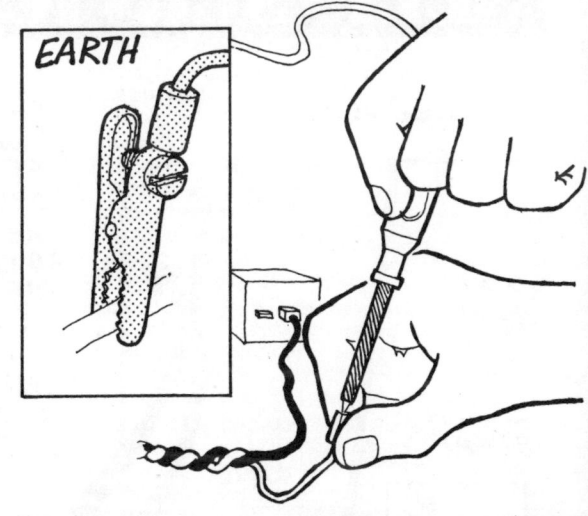

EARTH

IF A COMPONENT IS RECEIVING POWER, THE BULB IN THE CIRCUIT-TESTER SHOULD LIGHT WHEN THE CROCODILE CLIP IS ATTACHED TO A GOOD EARTH POINT AND THE PROBE TO THE COMPONENTS POWER SUPPLY WIRE OR CONNECTION.

TRACING ELECTRICAL FAULTS II

HEADLAMP

CAR BODY

EARTH STRAP

WING

BATTERY

HEADLAMPS AND HORNS AS WELL AS OTHER EQUIPMENT OFTEN SUFFER FROM BAD EARTHING. THIS IS BECAUSE THE CURRENT USUALLY HAS TO PASS (TO EARTH) THROUGH THE CAR BODY. ANY LOOSE OR RUSTY JOINTS OR PATCHES OF FILLER ALONG THE WAY CAN PREVENT THE COMPONENT EARTHING AND SO BREAKING THE CIRCUIT.

CORROSION

FILLER OR FIBREGLASS

POOR JOINT

TO EARTH

TO UNEARTHED BATTERY TERMINAL

TO CHECK THE EARTH RETURN OF A COMPONENT, CONNECT A TEST LAMP TO THE UNEARTHED BATTERY TERMINAL. THE BULB WILL THEN LIGHT IF THE OTHER WIRE IS CONNECTED WITH ANY EARTHED POINT.

TOUCH THE BODY OR EARTH POINT OF THE COMPONENT. IF THE TEST LAMP DOES NOT LIGHT, THE COMPONENT IS NOT EARTHED. TOUCH THE TEST WIRE ON POINTS BACK THROUGH EACH SECTION OF THE EARTH'S ROUTE TO THE BATTERY. WHEN YOU FIND THE JOINT WHERE THE INTERRUPTION TAKES PLACE, YOU CAN EITHER TAKE THE JOINT TO PIECES AND CLEAN IT OR CONNECT A PIECE OF WIRE TO THE BODY OF THE COMPONENT AND FIX IT TO A POINT WHERE THERE IS A GOOD EARTH. IN OTHER WORDS, PROVIDE A NEW EARTH.

SELF-SERVICING

BRAKES MUST BE ADJUSTED FROM TIME TO TIME TO MOVE THE BRAKE SHOES NEARER TO THE DRUM TO TAKE UP WEAR. DISC BRAKES ARE SELF-ADJUSTING

SIGNS & SYMPTOMS

IF YOUR BRAKES LACK STOPPING POWER, REQUIRE HEAVY PEDAL PRESSURE OR HAVE LONG PEDAL TRAVEL, THEY NEED ADJUSTING.

NOTE BRAKE SHOES SHOULD BE ADJUSTED WHEN THE DRUMS ARE COLD AND _NEVER_ ADJUST ONE WHEEL ALONE.

TOOLS FOR THE JOB

JACK, AXLE STANDS OR BLOCKS OF WOOD, CHOCKS AND BRAKE ADJUSTING SPANNER OR SCREWDRIVER

① APPLY THE HANDBRAKE. OR, IF WORKING ON A REAR WHEEL, FULLY RELEASE THE HANDBRAKE AND CHOCK THE CAR SECURELY

② JACK UP THE WHEEL UNTIL CLEAR OF THE GROUND AND TURN THE ADJUSTER UNTIL THE WHEEL LOCKS.

③ BACK OFF THE ADJUSTER JUST ENOUGH TO ALLOW THE WHEEL TO TURN FREELY.

④ REPEAT WITH THE OTHER THREE WHEELS AND TEST THE BRAKES.

ADJUSTERS VARY FROM CAR TO CAR. A & B ARE THE TWO MAIN TYPES.

Ⓐ DRUM OR BACKPLATE   ADJUSTERS   Ⓑ BACKPLATE

IN Ⓐ TURN THE WHEEL UNTIL THE HOLE IN THE DRUM (OR BACKPLATE) IS IN LINE WITH THE ADJUSTER. USING A SCREWDRIVER TURN THE SERRATED NUTS (USUALLY CLOCKWISE TO CLOSE).

IN Ⓑ TURN THE SQUARE OR HEXAGON HEAD (AGAIN USUALLY CLOCKWISE). ON THE FRONT BRAKES OF BOTH TYPES THERE IS USUALLY A SEPARATE ADJUSTER FOR EACH SHOE. THESE MUST BE ADJUSTED INDIVIDUALLY.

SELF-SERVICING

FIT A NEW EXHAUST SYSTEM

A BROKEN OR DECAYED EXHAUST SYSTEM IS NOISY, UNLAWFUL AND BAD FOR PERFORMANCE. BUT, MOST IMPORTANT, IT WILL ALLOW POISONOUS FUMES TO ENTER THE CAR. SO DON'T DELAY REPLACING A FAULTY EXHAUST.

BUY A NEW SET OF CLAMPS, HANGERS AND GASKET WITH YOUR SYSTEM. THESE ARE SOME COMMON TYPES OF FITTING USED—

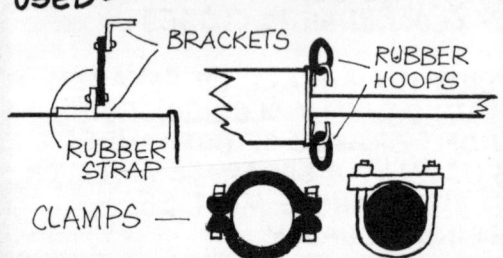

BRACKETS

RUBBER HOOPS

RUBBER STRAP

CLAMPS —

● PUT THE CAR UP ON RAMPS OR AXLE STANDS AND MAKE SECURE. BEFORE DISMANTLING THE OLD SYSTEM, SOAK ALL JOINTS, CLAMPS AND BRACKETS WITH RELEASING FLUID.

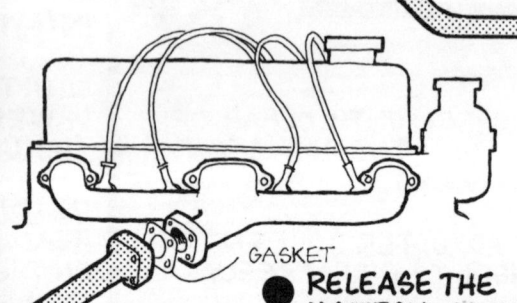

GASKET

● RELEASE THE MANIFOLD CONNECTION, UNDO THE STRAPS AND HANGERS AND REMOVE THE SYSTEM

SILENCER

● MANŒUVRE THE NEW SYSTEM INTO POSITION AND, WITH CLAMPS IN PLACE, FIT THE SECTIONS TOGETHER.
BEFORE YOU TIGHTEN THE CLAMPS CHECK THAT THE PIPES OR BOX WILL NOT HIT AGAINST ANYTHING.
FINALLY, MAKE SURE EVERY JOINT IS COMPLETELY SEALED AGAINST GAS LEAKS.

SELF-SERVICING

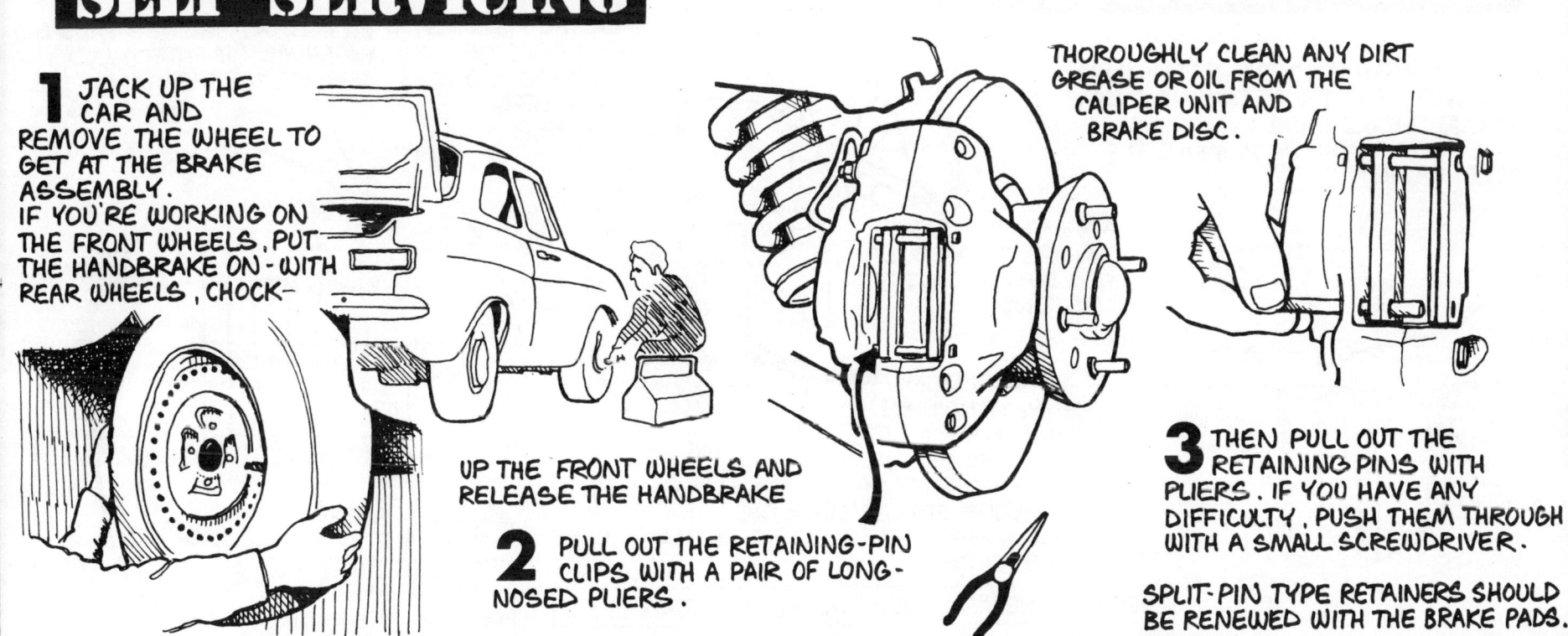

1 JACK UP THE CAR AND REMOVE THE WHEEL TO GET AT THE BRAKE ASSEMBLY. IF YOU'RE WORKING ON THE FRONT WHEELS, PUT THE HANDBRAKE ON - WITH REAR WHEELS, CHOCK-

UP THE FRONT WHEELS AND RELEASE THE HANDBRAKE

2 PULL OUT THE RETAINING-PIN CLIPS WITH A PAIR OF LONG-NOSED PLIERS.

THOROUGHLY CLEAN ANY DIRT GREASE OR OIL FROM THE CALIPER UNIT AND BRAKE DISC.

3 THEN PULL OUT THE RETAINING PINS WITH PLIERS. IF YOU HAVE ANY DIFFICULTY, PUSH THEM THROUGH WITH A SMALL SCREWDRIVER.

SPLIT-PIN TYPE RETAINERS SHOULD BE RENEWED WITH THE BRAKE PADS.

1 AFTER REMOVING THE RETAINING-PIN CLIPS AND THE RETAINING PINS, WITHDRAW THE OLD PADS AND SHIMS. WIGGLE THEM SLIGHTLY TO MAKE THE REMOVAL EASIER.

2 WITH THE PADS OUT, CLEAN RUST AND DIRT FROM THE PISTONS.

3 THE PISTONS MUST NOW BE MOVED BACK A LITTLE TO MAKE ROOM FOR THE NEW, THICKER, PADS. PUT YOUR FINGER OVER THE BLEED NIPPLE AND LOOSEN IT SO THAT FLUID CAN ESCAPE.

4 PUSH BACK THE PISTONS WITH A PIECE OF WOOD AND CLOSE THE BLEED NIPPLE.

5 INSERT THE NEW PADS AND SHIMS (IF FITTED) AND REPLACE THE RETAINING PINS AND CLIPS.

6 MAKE SURE THE BLEED NIPPLE IS TIGHT AND PUMP THE BRAKE TO POSITION THE PADS.

CHECK THE NEW PADS WITH THE OLD ONES FOR SIZE ETC.

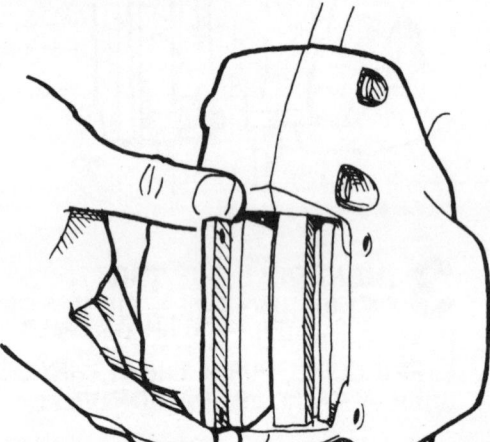

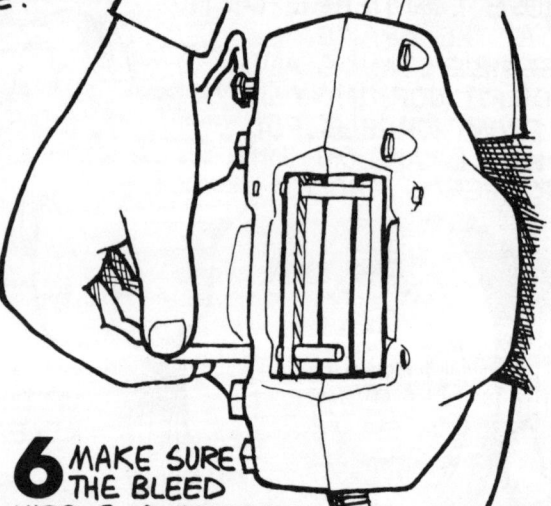

SELF-SERVICING

GREASE THE FRONT SUSPENSION

THE FRONT WHEELS MUST BE OFF THE GROUND FOR THE LUBRICATION TO BE EFFECTIVE.

USE AXLE STANDS AND MAKE SURE THE CAR IS SECURE IN THE TILTED POSITION AND THE REAR WHEELS ARE CHOCKED BEFORE GETTING UNDER.

CLEAN THE GREASE NIPPLES BEFORE APPLYING THE GUN.

RANGE ROVER

NIPPLE

NIPPLE

PUMP UNTIL FRESH GREASE COMES OUT OF THE SEALS. IF ANY GETS ON THE TYRES OR BRAKE HOSES, WIPE IT OFF IMMEDIATELY AS IT WILL PERISH THE RUBBER.

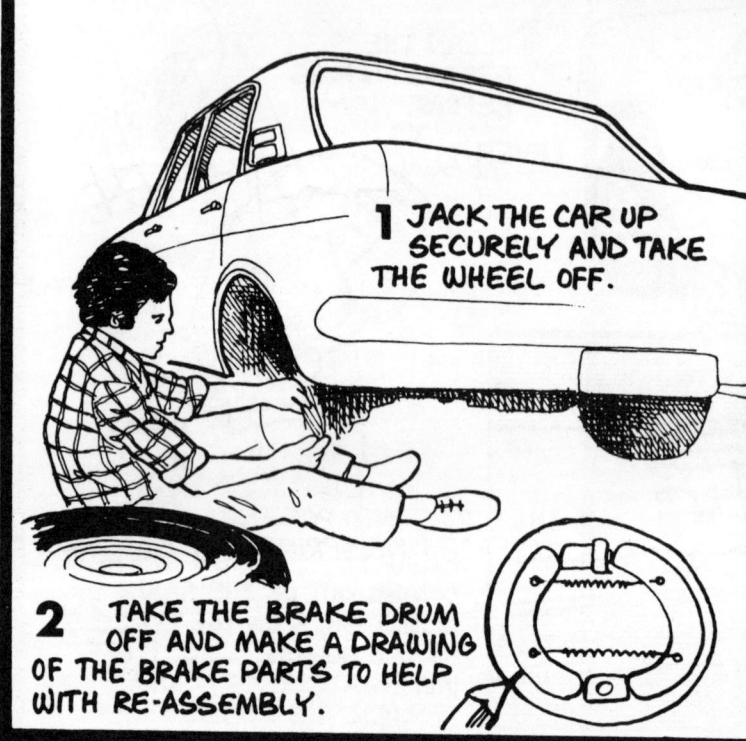

1 JACK THE CAR UP SECURELY AND TAKE THE WHEEL OFF.

2 TAKE THE BRAKE DRUM OFF AND MAKE A DRAWING OF THE BRAKE PARTS TO HELP WITH RE-ASSEMBLY.

3 UNDO EACH SPRING WASHER (TURN THROUGH

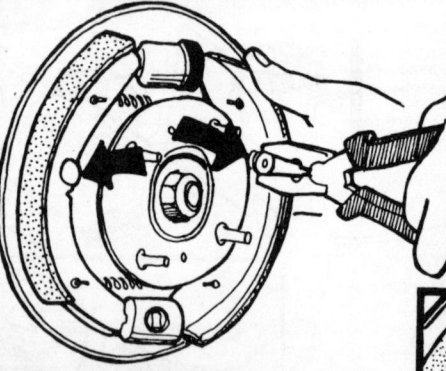

90° THEN SLIP IT OFF) HOLD-ING THE PIN BEHIND THE BACK PLATE TO PREVENT IT FALL-ING OUT.

REMOVE THE SPRING AND PULL THE PIN OUT THROUGH THE BACK PLATE.

4 USE A LARGE SCREW-DRIVER

TO LEVER OFF THE SHOES ONE AT A TIME.

5 TIE SOME WIRE OR PUT A RUBBER BAND ROUND THE WHEEL CYLINDER TO STOP FLUID RUNNING OUT.

SELF~SERVICING

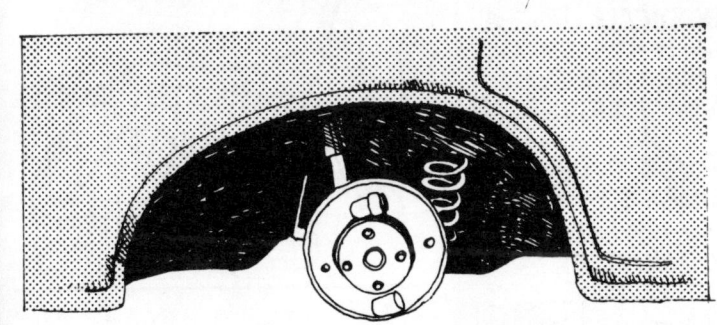

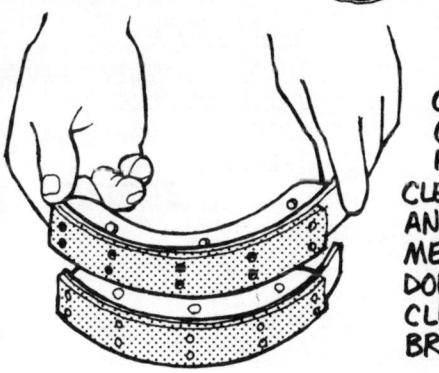

1 WITH THE OLD SHOES OFF, CHECK THE NEW ONES AGAINST THEM FOR SIZE AND TYPE. CLEAN THE BACK PLATE AND THE ADJUSTER MECHANISM. IF YOU'RE DOING A REAR WHEEL, CLEAN THE HANDBRAKE LINKAGE.

2 CONNECT THE NEW SHOES AND THEIR SPRINGS. CHECK YOUR SKETCH

FOR THE CORRECT POSITIONS OF THE SPRINGS. THEN PLACE ONE END OF EACH SHOE IN ITS ABUTMENT SLOT.

3 REMOVE THE WIRE FROM THE WHEEL CYLINDER AND LEVER

THE SHOES INTO POSITION. REPLACE PINS, SPRINGS AND WASHERS.

4 REPLACE THE DRUM. TIGHTEN THE ADJUSTER FULLY THEN SLACKEN OFF UNTIL THE DRUM IS JUST FREE. REPLACE THE WHEEL ETC.

SELF~SERVICING

DECOKE I: PREPARATION

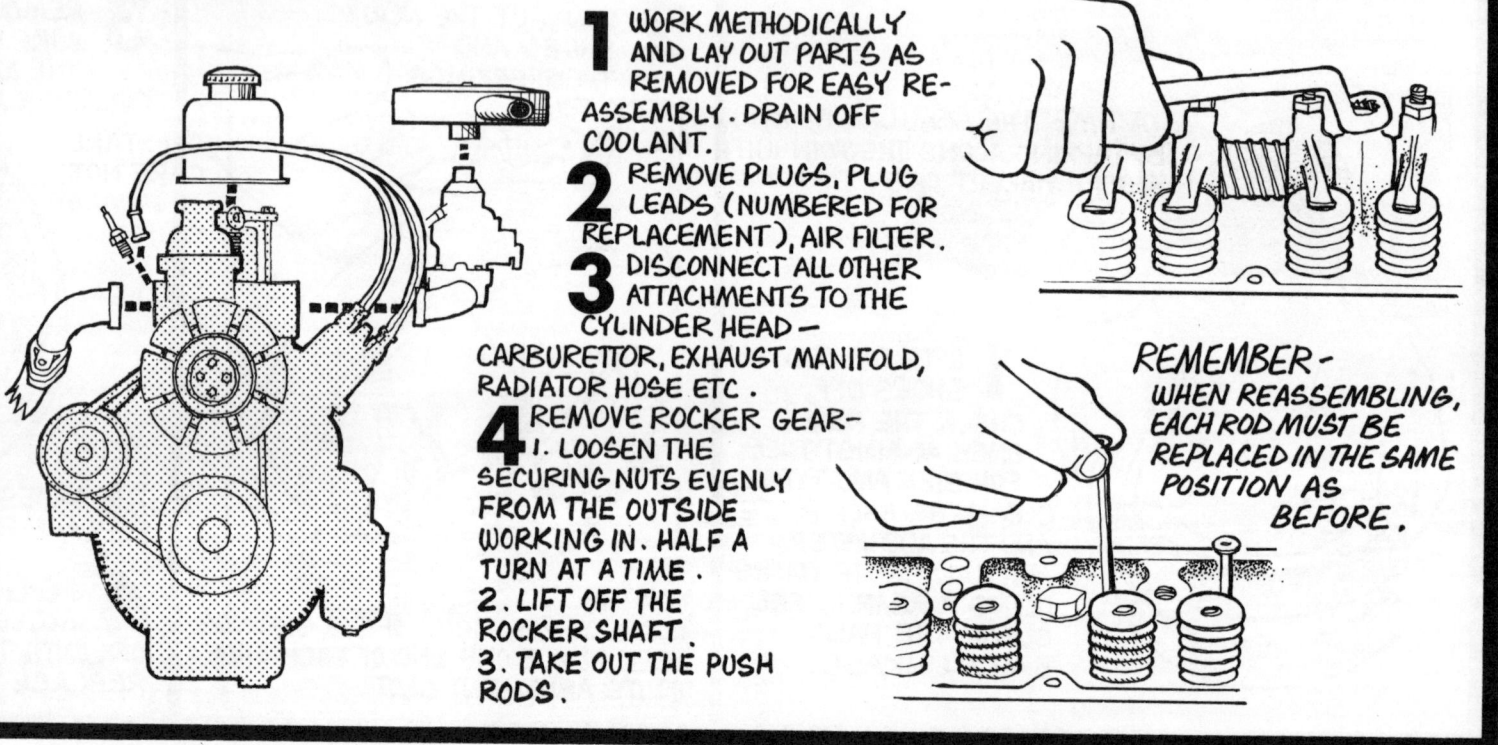

CARBON DEPOSIT BUILDS UP IN THE ENGINE ON THE PISTON CROWNS AND CYLINDER HEAD. THIS CAN CAUSE LOSS OF PERFORMANCE AND EXCESSIVE PINKING. CARBON IS RARELY A PROBLEM IN MODERN CARS, BUT IF YOU FIND YOURS NEEDS A DECOKE, HERE'S HOW →

TOOLS ETC:
GRINDING PASTE
VALVE GRINDING TOOL
VALVE COMPRESSOR
SOCKET SET
SPANNERS
TORQUE WRENCH
RAGS
PARAFFIN

1 WORK METHODICALLY AND LAY OUT PARTS AS REMOVED FOR EASY RE-ASSEMBLY. DRAIN OFF COOLANT.

2 REMOVE PLUGS, PLUG LEADS (NUMBERED FOR REPLACEMENT), AIR FILTER.

3 DISCONNECT ALL OTHER ATTACHMENTS TO THE CYLINDER HEAD — CARBURETTOR, EXHAUST MANIFOLD, RADIATOR HOSE ETC.

4 REMOVE ROCKER GEAR-
1. LOOSEN THE SECURING NUTS EVENLY FROM THE OUTSIDE WORKING IN. HALF A TURN AT A TIME.
2. LIFT OFF THE ROCKER SHAFT.
3. TAKE OUT THE PUSH RODS.

REMEMBER-
WHEN REASSEMBLING, EACH ROD MUST BE REPLACED IN THE SAME POSITION AS BEFORE.

SELF-SERVICING

DECOKE II: REMOVE CYLINDER HEAD

LOOSEN THE RETAINING NUTS HOLDING THE CYLINDER HEAD (SEE HANDBOOK FOR CORRECT ORDER) HALF A TURN AT A TIME. THE SEAL CAN BE BROKEN BY TAPPING ALONG THE JOIN WITH A SOFT MALLET OR BY TURNING THE ENGINE OVER.

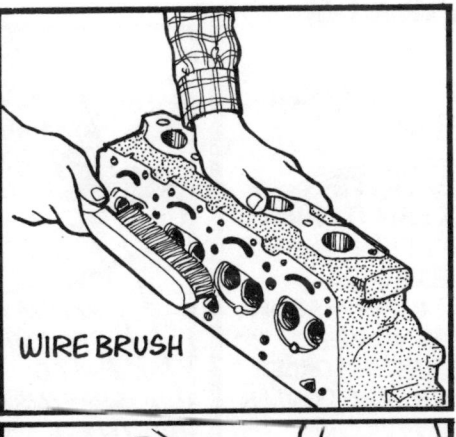

WIRE BRUSH

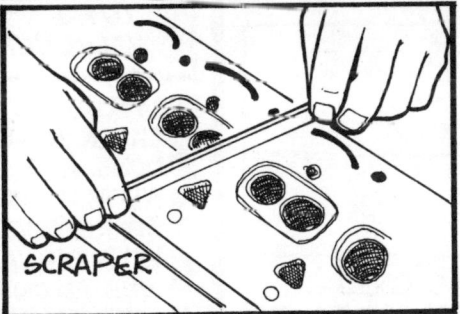

SCRAPER

THE CARBON DEPOSITS CAN NOW BE CLEANED OFF. TAKE CARE NOT TO DAMAGE FLAT SURFACES, ESPECIALLY IF THE HEAD IS OF LIGHT ALLOY

DRILL FITTED WITH WIRE BRUSH

START WITH A WIRE BRUSH BUT USE A WOODEN SCRAPER ON STUBBORN DEPOSITS IF NEEDED. AN ELECTRIC DRILL FITTED WITH WIRE BRUSHES CAN REALLY SPEED UP THE CLEANING OF EXHAUST AND INLET PORTS. A SLOWER ALTERNATIVE IS EMERY PAPER AND PARAFFIN. WASH THE SURFACES THOROUGHLY WITH PARAFFIN AFTER DECARBONISING.

SELF~SERVICING

DECOKE III: REMOVE VALVES

REMOVING THE VALVES FROM THE CYLINDER HEAD

AFTER DECARBONISING THE CYLINDER HEAD, CLEAN IT THOROUGHLY WITH PARAFFIN BEFORE STARTING ON THE VALVES.
USE A G-CLAMP COMPRESSOR TO REMOVE THE VALVES.
KEEP EACH ASSEMBLY IN ORDER FOR REPLACING IN SAME POSITION.

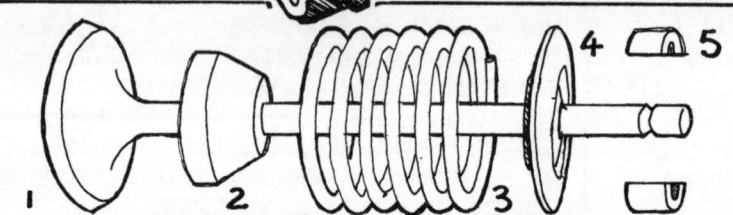

1 VALVE   2 OIL SEAL   3 SPRING   4 SPRING COLLAR
5 SPLIT COLLET   (ASSEMBLY VARIES FROM CAR TO CAR)

APPLY GRINDING PASTE SPARINGLY TO THE VALVE HEAD

GRINDING IN THE VALVES

1 SUPPORT THE HEAD ON BLOCKS.

2 CHECK THE VALVE SEATS. IF BADLY PITTED OR BURNT, GET THE JOB DONE AT A GARAGE.

3 ATTACH THE VALVE TO THE GRINDING TOOL AND APPLY PASTE SPARINGLY TO THE VALVE HEAD.

4 WITH THE VALVE IN POSITION IN ITS SEAT, ROTATE IT IN BOTH DIRECTIONS ALLOWING THE PASTE TO CUT AWAY UNEVENNESS ON EITHER SURFACE.

5 AFTER GRINDING, CLEAN ALL SURFACES WITH PARAFFIN. LUBRICATE STEMS & SEATS.

SELF-SERVICING

1 CLEAN BLOCK FACE AND SMEAR OIL INSIDE CYLINDER BORES.

2 CHECK NEW CYLINDER-HEAD GASKET AND PLACE ON CYLINDER BLOCK RIGHT SIDE UP.

3 PLACE CYLINDER HEAD ON GASKET AND SCREW RETAINING NUTS FINGER TIGHT.

TYPICAL CYLINDER-HEAD TIGHTENING SEQUENCE

4 TIGHTEN DOWN FURTHER ACCORDING TO SEQUENCE LAID DOWN BY THE CAR MANUFACTURER.

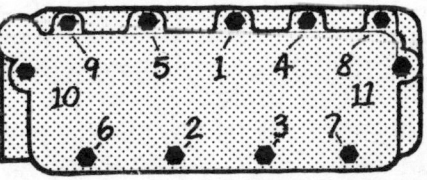

5 TIGHTEN, AGAIN, WITH A TORQUE WRENCH CORRECTLY SET AND ALSO IN SEQUENCE.

6 REFIT PUSH RODS THEN ROCKER SHAFT. TIGHTEN CAREFULLY AND EVENLY.

7 ADJUST TAPPETS.

8 CLEAN MANIFOLD AND REFIT WITH NEW GASKETS. TIGHTEN EVENLY.

9 REPLACE HOSES, CARBURETTOR AND OTHER HEAD ATTACHMENTS. FILL UP WITH COOLANT.

10 START THE ENGINE AND CHECK THAT OIL IS REACHING THE VALVE ROCKERS.

11 WHEN THE ENGINE IS THOROUGHLY WARM, TIGHTEN THE CYLINDER-HEAD NUTS WITH TORQUE WRENCH IN CORRECT SEQUENCE.

12 GIVE THE TAPPETS A FINAL ADJUSTMENT AND REPLACE ROCKER COVER (WITH A NEW GASKET).

13 ADJUST CARBURETTOR AND IGNITION AS REQUIRED. CHECK FOR LEAKS.

AFTER 500 MILES RE-TIGHTEN CAST IRON CYLINDER HEAD (AND OTHERS, IF RECOMMENDED BY MANUFACTURER).

ADJUST TAPPETS AND VALVE CLEARANCES

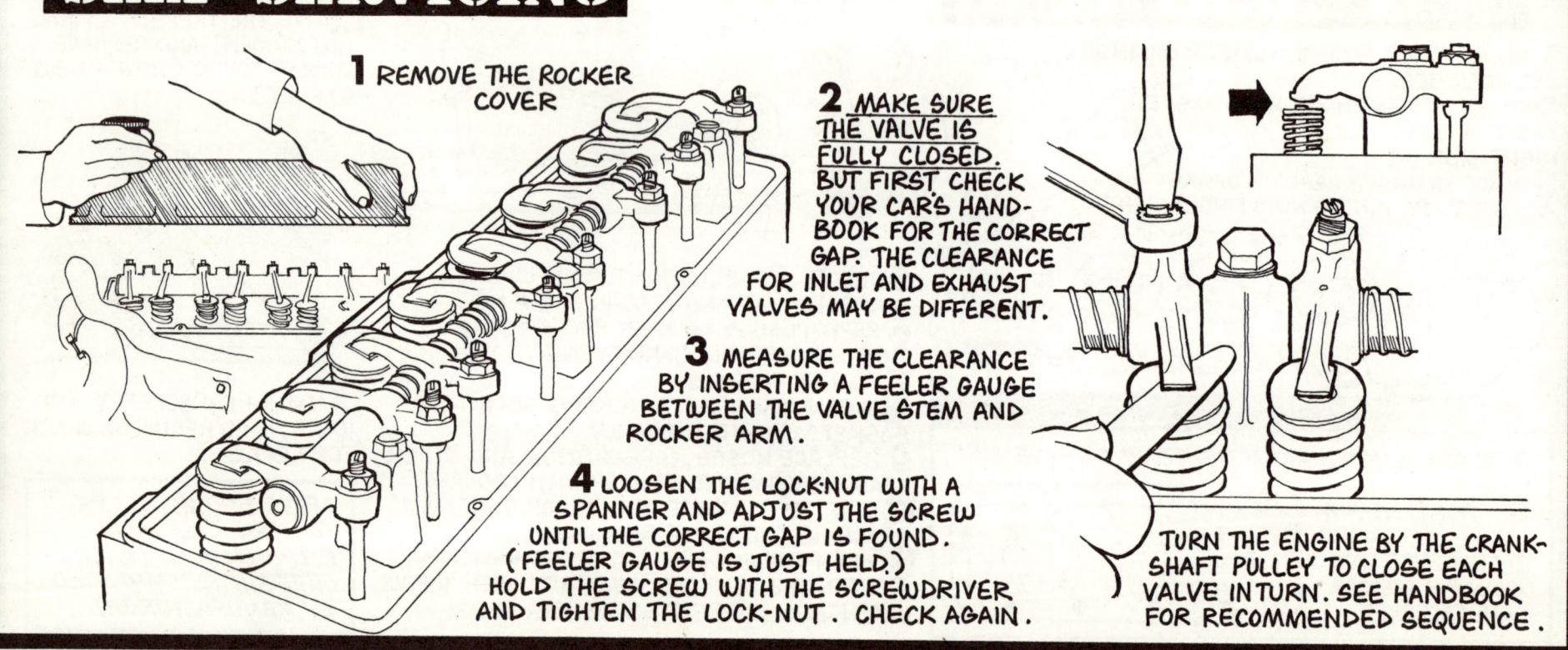

1 REMOVE THE ROCKER COVER

2 <u>MAKE SURE THE VALVE IS FULLY CLOSED.</u> BUT FIRST CHECK YOUR CAR'S HAND-BOOK FOR THE CORRECT GAP. THE CLEARANCE FOR INLET AND EXHAUST VALVES MAY BE DIFFERENT.

3 MEASURE THE CLEARANCE BY INSERTING A FEELER GAUGE BETWEEN THE VALVE STEM AND ROCKER ARM.

4 LOOSEN THE LOCK-NUT WITH A SPANNER AND ADJUST THE SCREW UNTIL THE CORRECT GAP IS FOUND. (FEELER GAUGE IS JUST HELD.) HOLD THE SCREW WITH THE SCREWDRIVER AND TIGHTEN THE LOCK-NUT . CHECK AGAIN .

TURN THE ENGINE BY THE CRANK-SHAFT PULLEY TO CLOSE EACH VALVE IN TURN. SEE HANDBOOK FOR RECOMMENDED SEQUENCE .